Planet Friendly Publishing
✔ Made in the United States
✔ Printed on Recycled Paper
  Text: 10%   Cover: 10%
Learn more: www.greenedition.org

GREEN
EDITION

At Dover Publications we're committed to producing books in an earth-friendly manner and to helping our customers make greener choices.

Manufacturing books in the United States ensures compliance with strict environmental laws and eliminates the need for international freight shipping, a major contributor to global air pollution.

And printing on recycled paper helps minimize our consumption of trees, water and fossil fuels. The text of *Ideal Homes of the Thirties* was printed on paper made with 10% post-consumer waste, and the cover was printed on paper made with 10% post-consumer waste. According to Environmental Defense's Paper Calculator, by using this innovative paper instead of conventional papers, we achieved the following environmental benefits:

Trees Saved: 6 • Air Emissions Eliminated: 498 pounds
Water Saved: 2,397 gallons • Solid Waste Eliminated: 145 pounds

For more information on our environmental practices, please visit us online at www.doverpublications.com/green

IDEAL HOMES

of the Thirties

WITH A NEW INTRODUCTION BY DANIEL D. REIFF

DOVER PUBLICATIONS, INC.

MINEOLA, NEW YORK

Copyright

Introduction to the Dover edition copyright © 2010 by Daniel D. Reiff
All rights reserved.

Bibliographical Note

This Dover edition, first published in 2010, is an unabridged republication of the eleventh edition of *Ideal Homes: Two-Story Houses*, originally published by the Plan Service Company, St. Paul, Minnesota, ca. 1933. The illustrations, floor plans, and accompanying text for the sixty house designs have been rearranged as two-page spreads to better fit the trim size of the present volume. A new introduction by Daniel D. Reiff has been specially prepared for this edition.

Library of Congress Cataloging-in-Publication Data

Ideal homes.
    Ideal homes of the thirties / with a new introduction by Daniel D. Reiff.—Dover ed.
        p. cm.
    Originally published: Ideal homes : two-story houses. 11th ed. St. Paul, Minn. : Plan Service Co., ca. 1933.
    Includes bibliographical references.
    ISBN-13: 978-0-486-47255-3
    ISBN-10: 0-486-47255-8
    1. Architecture, Domestic—United States—Designs and plans. 2. Architecture—United States—History—20th century—Designs and plans. I. Plan Service Company (Saint Paul, Minn.) II. Title.
NA7208.I32 2010
728.0973—dc22

                                                                2009029287

Manufactured in the United States by Courier Corporation
47255801
www.doverpublications.com

Introduction to the Dover Edition

by Daniel D. Reiff, Ph.D.

*I*N THE FIRST HALF of the twentieth century, a middle- or upper-middle-class family who wanted to have an attractive, well-designed six- or seven-room house built for themselves had a number of choices. Although one's first inclination might be to "consult an architect or builder," there were in fact a number of options—some quite economical—open to them, thanks to the printed book.

One of the most popular routes was to consult a catalog of house-plans published by one of the many mail-order plan companies, and order their plans and specifications for the preferred dwelling. The first mail-order plans for houses seem to be those advertised by Cleaveland, Backus and Backus in their 1856 book of house designs, *Village and Farm Cottages*. Other such volumes soon followed. Books of plans were published by Cummings and Miller in 1865; in the 1870s by George Palliser and also E. C. Hussey; in the 1880s books of house designs by R. W. Shoppell, and George F. Barber became popular. By 1898 one of the most prolific companies, a Chicago firm which became known as The Radford Architectural Company, was offering great numbers of appealing mail-order house plans. In the early twentieth century there were a vast number of such firms: Standard Homes Company of Washington, D.C. (beginning about 1921) and Home Builders Catalog Co., Chicago (beginning in 1926). These two were among the most popular and prolific, each publishing hundreds of plans.[1] The designs provided could be for frame, for face brick (on frame construction), solid brick, or concrete dwellings. The Plan Service Company of St. Paul, Minnesota, was one of this legion of mail-order plan companies serving a national audience.

Just when the Plan Service Company was established is hard to pin down, since the catalogs are rare nowadays, and nothing about the company is provided in their front matter. An *Ideal Homes* catalog from 1923 is in the Library of Congress; a copy from 1926 is at the University of Minnesota Library;[2] this copy from my own collection appears to have been issued in the mid-1940s—but with 14 designs that are carried over from earlier *Ideal Homes* catalogs.[3] Since this one is the "eleventh edition," they seem to have been issued every couple of years, and been a mainstay during the 1930s. These were especially attractive publications: in the 1926 Minnesota copy, all 30 plates (plus the title-page dwelling) were in color; and in this catalog, containing 60 designs, half of them are in color, with the rest in sepia.

The designs in this *Ideal Homes* "Two-Story Houses" catalog are all "up-to-date" popular house types, illustrated with a photograph of the dwelling as built. English country houses and cottages were the most numerous, followed by two-story American Colonials, and then one-and-a half-story American Colonials—with an admixture of California-Spanish, Italianate, and Vernacular. There is one Dutch Colonial (pp. 6–7) and a Stickley Bungalow (pp. 116–117), both 1920s holdovers; other "unique" types are a palatial "Greek Revival" (pp. 18–19), and a variant of International Modern (pp. 106–107). As outlined on pages 122–123, the prospective home builder could order the "complete working plans, details, and specifications" for any of these plans for prices ranging from $12.25 (design 438) to $28.75 (design 424)—the increases dependent on the size of the house.[4]

Catalogs of house plans, like these in the *Ideal Homes* compendium, were extremely popular. But where did such companies get their plans? One source would have been the various building materials organizations. These organizations, to encourage homeowners and builders to use their specific product, frequently sponsored competitions for house designs, and published countless catalogs of the resulting designs (whose plans could be ordered by mail) themselves—or contributed the results quietly to house-plan companies. For example, The Association of American Portland Cement (Philadelphia) held such a competition in 1907; in a 1910 house-plan catalog the Building Brick Association of America states that the plans were "a selection from more than 800 drawings submitted in a competition," and their plan catalog of 1912 drew its designs from 666 entries in a competition. Almost every building-trade organization of the day held competitions for house designs of various sizes, as mentioned in their house-plan catalogs, for example: National Fire Proofing Co., Philadelphia, 1912; Hydraulic-Press Brick Co., St. Louis, 1914;

American Face Brick Association, Chicago, 1920; United States Gypsum Co., Chicago, 1925; California Redwood Association, San Francisco, 1925; Weyerhaeuser Forest Products, St. Paul, 1926. From their catalogs one could purchase low-priced plans and specifications of the houses illustrated—featuring their particular product, of course.[5]

Sometimes house-plan competitions were sponsored by newspapers, such as the *Chicago Tribune,* which held a national competition[6] for house plans in 1926, and in 1927 published a handsome volume of 99 skillfully-drawn designs, for five- and six-room houses, that could be built for about $7,500—a fairly substantial sum in those days, but affordable to middle- and upper-middle-class families.[7]

What is interesting to discover is that the Plan Service Company of St. Paul, Minnesota, seems not to have been a large company, but rather to have been the work of one man—not a stable of designers or architects! A search in selected copies of the city directories of St. Paul reveals that there were no listings for the "Plan Service Company" in 1923, 1928, 1933–39, 1944, or 1946; but the address given for the company (which was the same on the 1926 catalog as for the current mid-1940s version) was the residence of one Charles W. Battley! His occupation was listed as "publisher, Public Service Magazine;" and in some directories he is identified as an "advertising agent."[8] Thus the mail-order plan business was just one aspect of his advertising and "public service" activities. But where did he get these attractive, and consistently presented, designs, if he did not have (like Radford) his own architects preparing them?

A possible explanation for this is suggested by editorial matter in the 1927 edition of the Chicago *Home Builders Catalog* (p. 633): The editors state that the catalog was produced "by the same men who for 12 years have conducted the Architectural & Publicity Bureau—the Bureau whose plan service is used by eleven of the leading Retail Lumber Associations of America." Thus there was at least one major trade group (not just the building supply companies themselves) that prepared and shared these house plans—and over the years could develop small house plans that were nearly perfect in style, design, and appeal. It must have been from such a group that Battley obtained his designs.

Battley's attractive and colorful catalogs seem to have been reasonably popular, for the original title page of this copy advertises others in this series. His volume on "Low-Cost

House in Potsdam, New York, probably built from *Ideal Homes* design number 418, pages 104–105 (Photo by the author).

Bungalows" was in its 13th edition; "Medium-Priced Bungalows" in its 12th; and two new offerings were available, "Popular-Priced Bungalows" and "De Luxe Bungalows" both in their first editions. Although the current *Ideal Homes* "Two-Story Houses" catalog provided only one ground plan for each illustrated design,[9] three of these other volumes give the prospective homeowner a choice in interior configurations. The plans in *Ideal Homes* all appear to be professionally prepared; those from the early years (1920s) have a slightly different style of drafting and lettering, but are indeed uniform; those from the 400 series are more "modern" in lettering and graphic treatment.

Now that this catalog is reprinted, it is likely that houses built following its designs will be located. One dwelling that, at least from the outside, appears to be based on design 418 (pp. 104–105) can be seen in Potsdam, New York.[10] However, a prospective homeowner did not really have to purchase a set of house plans; he could simply take one of these designs—from this, or any of the various of house-plan catalogs of the day—to a local builder or contractor! They could easily work up specifications from the details and dimensions given on each plate, and thus build a "bootleg" copy of the original design.

I can illustrate one instance of this. A house in Fredonia, New York, erected in 1941–42, follows the *Ideal Homes* design 407 (pp. 60–61) closely, though with a few minor changes: the upstairs central dormer is omitted, the garage is given a gabled roof (Fredonia gets heavy snowfalls), the side screen porch is eliminated (the lot size does not leave room for one), and a different "stock" front door-casing is used. But the fact that design 407 was used seems certain, not only in the closeness of the finished design, but because the original plantings are in the same location,[11] and appear as they would with 40 years of growth! The builder, however, even if he consulted the plate in the *Ideal Homes* catalog, did not order the plans. The Fredonia house is different in size (32' 4" wide by 23' 2" deep, versus 30' square for design 407); and the floor plans are entirely different! Clearly, the homeowner selected an appealing design, and in concert with the builder, prepared a plan that fit their particular needs.

This was, after all, how house designs in books had been used in America since 1738, when Drayton Hall was erected following a plate in Palladio's *Quattro Libri*; how Samuel McIntire used plates in pattern books by Asher Benjamin and William Pain to create his

House in Fredonia, New York, copied from *Ideal Homes* design number 407, pages 60–61 (Photo by the author).

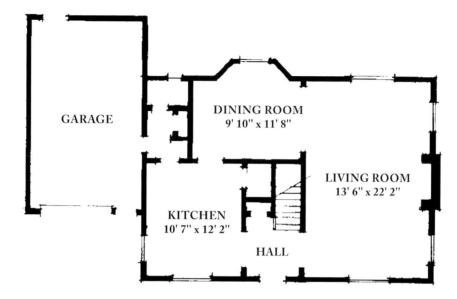

Plan of the Fredonia house, as built, 1941–42 (Plan by the author).

Gardner House in 1804; and how countless builders and carpenters copied—freely or meticulously—A. J. Downing's famous gothic cottage design of 1842 all across America, prior to the era of mail-order plans.

Whether one purchased plans and specifications from a house-plan catalog, or had a local contractor draw up his own plans based on the illustration and erect a copy—or variant—of the model,[12] one could be assured of an attractive professional design that would stand the test of time. With so many such houses in our neighborhoods today—still enjoyed and appreciated by their current occupants—the esthetic judgments of decades ago seem to have been correct.

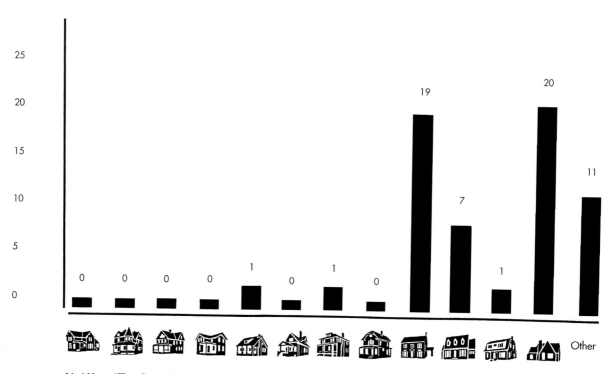

Ideal Homes "Two-Story Houses" catalog, 11th edition: house type distribution (logos and graph by Mark V. Stress).

Notes

1. The Standard Homes Company 1925 catalog, *Better Homes at Lower Cost: 101 Modern Home Standardized* [i.e., using standard length of lumber where possible, to save costs], was reprinted by Dover Publications in 1999 as *101 Classic Homes of the Twenties* (ISBN 0-486-40731-4).

2. This copy, entitled *Ideal Homes, 1926 Edition*, is in the collection of the Northwest Architectural Archives, Andersen Library, University of Minnesota, Minneapolis. An oblong volume (7 by 10½ inches), it consists of thirty house designs—photographs of the houses as erected—with plans and brief text on the facing page, plus a title page, and Price List page. My thanks to librarian Barbara Bezat for providing me with a xerographic copy of the complete catalog.

3. I believe that the *Ideal Homes* catalog being reprinted here dates from the mid-1940s (even if it include some designs from the 1920s) since the address for the Plan Service Company includes its postal zone, and these were not initiated until 1943. The title page's "modern" sans-serif typeface is also a mode common by the 1940s (Sears' house catalogs began using it in 1934); and in most of the 400 series designs, comments about installing air-conditioning again suggests a post-World War II era. The designs in this catalog which are clearly "older" are nos. 1, 7, 8, 11, 12, 15, 17, 20, 22, 36, 52, 74, 94, and 138; those featured in the 1926 catalog are nos. 8, 36, 52, 94, and 138. The illustrations are identical to those in the earlier catalog, and all are reproduced in color.

4. The prices for plans in the post-war 1940s version of the catalog are generally *lower* than those of the same design in the palmy prosperous days of the 1920s. For example, plans for design 8 cost $30 in 1926, but here are only $19; design 36 was then $30, but here only $16.50; and no. 94, formerly $25, is now $15.

5. These trade-company house plans were spread about widely—not just in their own publications. The Home Owners Institute's *Book of a Thousand Homes* (New York: 1927) states (in their acknowledgements, p. 5) that trade organizations "which have co-operated in supplying plans include: American Face Brick Association, Portland Cement Association, Common Brick Manufacturers Association of the United States, The Curtis Companies, Hollow Building Tile Manufacturers Association, National Lumber Manufacturers Association, Associated Metal Lath Manufacturers, Long Bell Lumber Company, and Lehigh Portland Cement Company."

6. The *Tribune* competition received entries from all over the country: California, Connecticut, Florida, Illinois, Indiana, Maine, Massachusetts, Michigan, Missouri, New Jersey, New York, North Carolina, North Dakota, Ohio, Oregon, Pennsylvania, Washington, and Wisconsin. The *Tribune* book was reprinted by Dover Publications in 2008 as *Elegant Small Homes of the Twenties: 99 Designs from a Competition* (ISBN 0-486-46910-7).

7. At first glance this seems like a preposterously low amount for a house, but because of inflation, and the great rise in Americans' standard of living, the dollar in those days was obviously "worth more" than today. For example (drawing from a 1926 *National Geographic*—the year that the competition was advertised) we find that a four-door Dodge sedan cost $895 to $995; a Chrysler was $1,395 to $1,895; and a Cadillac cost $2,995. Though naturally automotive amenities are different today, multiplying by 12 give a rough idea of current costs; thus the $7,500 house would be about $90,000 today. Only the three prize-winning designs were available in cheap mail-order plans from the *Tribune*; for all others the reader would have to write to the designing architect (whose address was included with their drawings).

8. My thanks to Reference Librarian Hampton Smith of the Minnesota Historical Society for searching the St. Paul City Directories of these dates for information on the "Plan Service Company" and its owner.

9. While the designs in this volume provide only one floor plan for each house, oddly enough the Foreword says that "in some instances two or more floor plans" are given! This text must have been carried over erroneously from earlier editions; in the 1926 catalog, for example, 25 of the 30 designs had alternate plans, occasionally of different sizes, not just a different interior room configuration.

10. The house is located at 67½ Pierrepont Street; only an examination of the floor plan, however, would tell if it is based on the *Ideal Homes* plan, or a similar one from a rival company.

11. This photograph of the Toomey House, on Temple Street in Fredonia, was taken prior to 1987, at which time the plantings were all removed and the house re-landscaped.

12. Another source of images of well-designed houses as models for such "bootleg" copies would be the catalogs of companies that sold precut houses, such as Aladdin (the originator of the process in 1906), Sears, Roebuck, and Co., Bennett Homes, Gordon-Van Tine Co., and the like. These catalogs too provided exterior designs and floor plans, and also, often, interior views. Some of these have been reprinted by Dover Publications: the *Aladdin Homes "Built in a Day" Catalog No. 29, 1917* was reprinted in 1995 as *Aladdin "Built in a Day" House Catalog, 1917* (ISBN 0-486-28591-X); the 1926 Sears *Honor Bilt Modern Homes* catalog was reprinted in 1991 as *Small Houses of the Twenties* (ISBN 0-486-26709-1); and the 1923 *Gordon-Van Tine Homes* catalog was reprinted in 1992 as *117 House Designs of the Twenties* (ISBN 0-486-26959-0).

Daniel D. Reiff, Ph.D., is the author of *Houses from Books: Treatises, Pattern Books, and Catalogs in American Architecture, 1738–1950, A History and Guide* (Pennsylvania State University Press, 2000), which won the 2001 Historic Preservation Book Prize from the Center for Historic Preservation, Mary Washington College, Fredericksburg, Virginia.

Foreword

THE HOMES illustrated in this book are from actual photographs, which combine beauty, convenience and economy and bring to you the very latest in style and design of practical up-to-the-minute architecture. Your home is the reflection of your personality and the expression of your ideas, and with this thought in mind, it is hoped that the suggestions carried out in the interior and exterior planning of the homes shown herein will assist you in selecting a design conforming to your individual taste and requirements.

The proper selection of shrubbery adds wonderfully to the artistic appearance of any home, and in these illustrations we have endeavored to show how the placing of flowers, shrubbery, well located trees, a vine on a trellis—little touches that the homeowner can do himself to make a charming spot, though the house itself be small, even plain.

In the preparation of this book, great care has been exercised in selecting these types of homes that are in great demand and that can be constructed simply and economically by any competent carpenter or contractor. The interiors have been carefully and thoughtfully planned and excellent results have been accomplished in the number and size of rooms provided, considering the outside dimensions.

Alternative Floor Plans

To further assist you in the selection of a plan best suited to your requirements, both as to size and room arrangement, we have in some instances shown two or more floor plans for each house design illustrated. After selecting a suitable design, as to the exterior appearance, you should then decide definitely on the number of rooms required. To determine proper size of the various rooms, it would be advisable to measure the rooms in your present home and then compare with measurements shown on plan. If you desire to increase the size of a certain room by diminishing the size of another, it is a very simple matter for the carpenter or contractor to change location of partition walls. This same suggestion applies to location of windows and doors.

In planning the interiors, we have endeavored to make the arrangement of rooms thoroughly practical and convenient from every standpoint and to utilize every inch of floor space. The homes are all planned in a most economical way so as to eliminate the use of any material not absolutely required and for this reason it is advisable to conform to the outside dimensions of plans shown.

IDEAL HOMES

of the Thirties

Design No. 428

2

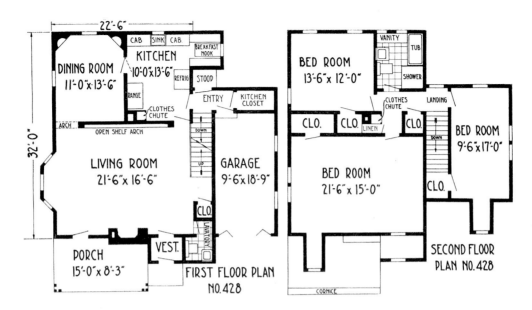

Plan No. 428—Size, 22½ by 32 feet

The sloping roof extending over porch, artistic dormers, gabled projection and attached garage at side give this very attractive semi-bungalow type home individuality in design with a rich and inviting appearance. Entry is made through vestibule into spacious living room having fireplace, French door to porch, triple bay windows, stairway to second floor, coat closet, lavatory adjoining, and triple arches along rear wall, the center one being recessed and having open shelves for books and ornamental pieces, with openings at either end, to dining room and to kitchen. The dining room has recessed corner arches. The kitchen is strictly modern, having cabinet with sink in center, chimney for range, clothes chute, refrigerator space, breakfast nook, rear entry adjoining with kitchen closet and doors to garage, basement and outdoors. The second floor arrangement includes three bedrooms, hall closet, clothes chute, linen closet and bathroom with tub, shower and built-in vanity with wall space for mirror between two casement windows. Exterior walls are covered with siding. Seven-foot basement under entire house with space for recreation room, toilet, laundry, furnace, vegetable and storage rooms. Ceiling height, first floor, 8 feet 3 inches; second floor, 8 feet.

Design No. 1

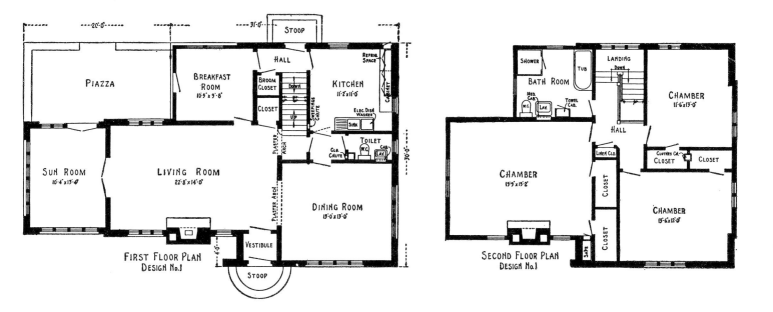

FIRST FLOOR PLAN
DESIGN No.1

PIAZZA

BREAKFAST ROOM
10'-9" x 9'-8"

HALL

KITCHEN
11'-2" x 11'-0"

BROOM CLOSET

CLOSET

STOOP

REFRIG. SPACE

ELEC. DISH WASHER

SINK

TOILET

W.C.

CLO. CHUTE

SUN ROOM
10'-4" x 13'-6"

LIVING ROOM
22'-8" x 14'-0"

DINING ROOM
15'-0" x 13'-0"

VESTIBULE

STOOP

SECOND FLOOR PLAN
DESIGN No.1

SHOWER

BATH ROOM

TUB

LANDING

CHAMBER
11'-6" x 13'-0"

W.C.

LAV.

HALL

CHAMBER
15'-5" x 15'-2"

LINEN CLO.

CLOSET

CLOTHES CLO.

CLOSET

CLOSET

CLOSET

CHAMBER
15'-6" x 12'-0"

This English type home with its unusual commanding appearance, combining stateliness, stability and individuality is all that the word beautiful implies. Entrance is made through vestibule into a spacious living room, having a very attractive fireplace, French doors leading to sunroom and breakfast room, plaster arch openings to dining room and hall, all combining to produce a palatial and most magnificent interior. A large kitchen is included in the arrangement with the most modern fixtures and conveniences. The second floor arrangement is very spacious, with extra large rooms and clothes closets, center hall connecting all rooms, extra large bathroom with tile floor and walls, equipped with shower, towel cabinet and electric heater built in wall. The owner's chamber has an attractive design fireplace, two closets and extra closet space that may be utilized for safe or cedar closet. The third floor has ample space for maids' room and bath. Seven-foot basement extends under entire house, with large recreation room fitted with fireplace. Boiler, laundry, toilet, fruit and storage rooms are also provided. No detail has been omitted in the planning of this home to make it thoroughly modern and up-to-date in every particular, both interior and exterior. The exterior is brick, with stucco trim and slate roof. The house is 30 feet in depth by 51 feet in width.

Design No. 36

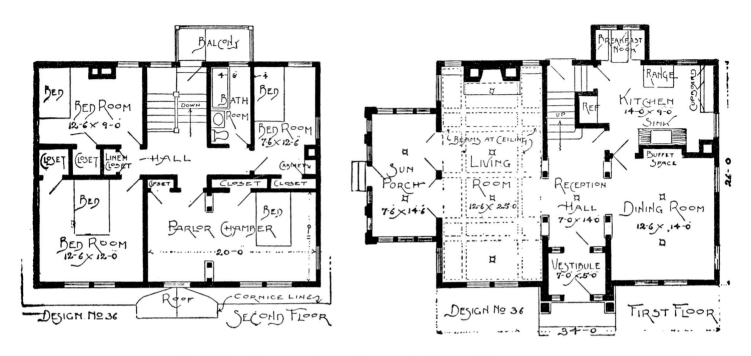

Design No. 36 — Second Floor

Design No. 36 — First Floor

This exceptionally classy Dutch Colonial house is 34 feet in width by 26 feet in depth, exclusive of sun porch. The interior planning is all that could be desired for this style home. The large living room with fireplace, French doors leading to sun porch, large reception hall with grand colonial staircase, vestibule and large dining room, all combine to produce a most magnificent interior. The kitchen is provided with cupboard, chimney for range, breakfast nook, and door to grade landing, leading to basement and outside. The second floor arrangement is very convenient and attractive, having four bedrooms, including the parlor chamber, each room having large closets, and connecting with center hall. A brick water table extends around entire house, with wide lap siding above. Basement under entire house, equipped with laundry tubs, vegetable cellar, and dust-proof coal bin. Hot water heat is recommended. Height of ceilings: First floor, 9 feet; second floor, 8 feet.

7

Design No. 422

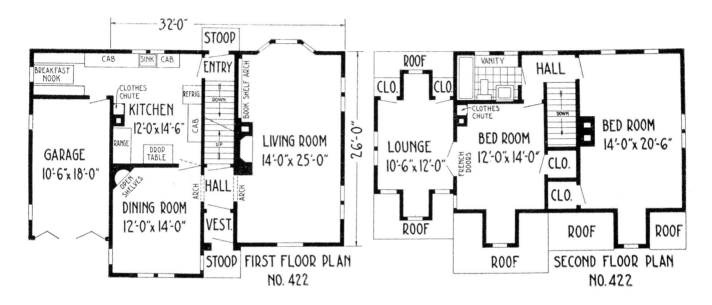

Plan No. 422—Size, 32 by 26 feet

This attractive semi-bungalow is very unique in design and a very popular modern type. Entrance is made through vestibule to small center hall with stairway to second floor and arched openings to living room and dining room. The living room is very spacious and well lighted and has a fireplace and recessed arch opening with open shelves for books or ornamental pieces. The kitchen is very complete with a cabinet having sink in center and another cabinet with refrigerator space, chimney for range, clothes chute, breakfast nook adjoining, door to garage and door to rear entry leading to basement and outdoors. Two good size bedrooms are located on second floor with a lounge adjoining one of the rooms. The bathroom has a clothes chute and built-in vanity with wall space for mirror between two casement windows. Seven-foot basement under entire house with space for recreation room, toilet, laundry, furnace, vegetable and storage rooms. Hot water heating plant with oil burner equipment is recommended. Air-conditioning equipment may be installed if desired. Ceiling height, first floor, 8 feet 3 inches; second floor, 8 feet.

Design No. 425

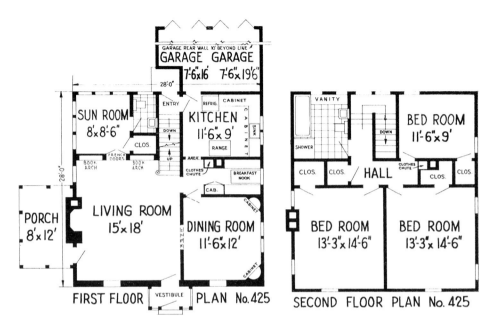

Plan No. 425—Size, 28 by 28 feet

The combination stone and siding front wall, glazed vestibule with copper roof and artistic design of side porch combine to produce the luxurious exterior of this attractive home. The vestibule entry leads to large living room having fireplace, French door to side porch and to sunroom with recessed arches on each side, stairway to second floor and door to breakfast nook. The sunroom has a coat closet and lavatory adjoining. The kitchen is modern in every respect, having cabinet with sink and window opening in center and refrigerator space at end, chimney for range, breakfast nook adjoining with cabinet and clothes chute, door to two-car garage and door to rear entry leading to basement and outdoors. The second floor arrangement includes three bedrooms, clothes chute, half closet, and bathroom with built-in vanity with wall space for mirror between two casement windows. The exterior walls are of siding except stone portion of front wall. Seven-foot basement under entire house with space for recreation room, toilet, laundry, furnace, vegetable and storage rooms. Hot water heating plant with oil burner equipment is recommended. Air-conditioning equipment may be installed. Ceiling height, first floor, 8 feet 3 inches; second floor, 8 feet.

Design No. 22

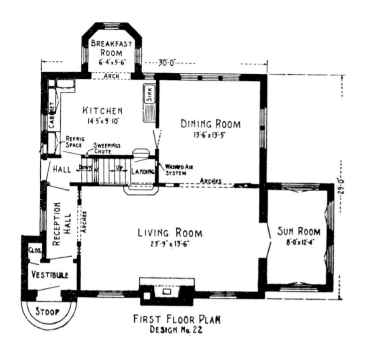

FIRST FLOOR PLAN
DESIGN No. 22

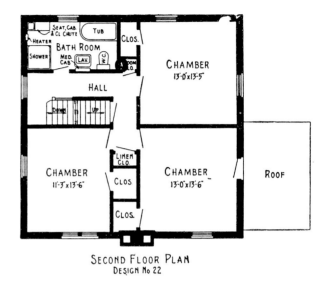

SECOND FLOOR PLAN
DESIGN No. 22

This strictly new type home embodies the English design so much in demand today. The house is 30 feet in width by 29 feet in depth, exclusive of the sunroom, breakfast room and vestibule projections. Entrance is made through vestibule to reception hall with triple plaster arch opening to living room, which is provided with fireplace, French doors leading to sunroom and triple plaster arch opening to dining room. The kitchen is very spacious and thoroughly up-to-date, having ample cabinet space, sweepings chute, breakfast room projection, door to landing, leading to second floor, also door to grade entry hall. The second floor arrangement includes three large bedrooms, each having large closets and connected to center hall, which has a linen and broom closet, also door to stairway, leading to third floor, where maid's room, bath, cedar and storage closets are provided. Seven-foot basement under entire house, with boiler, vegetable, laundry and recreation room.

Design No. 17

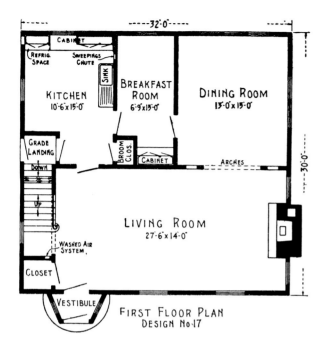

FIRST FLOOR PLAN
DESIGN No. 17

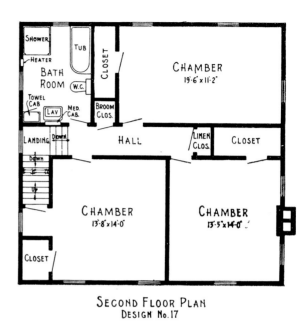

SECOND FLOOR PLAN
DESIGN No. 17

This Colonial home is 32 feet in width by 30 feet in depth. The interior arrangement is very spacious and embodies all the latest features of the up-to-date home, with exceptional large living room, having fireplace and triple plaster arch opening into dining room, cozy breakfast room with cabinets, and thoroughly modern kitchen having ample cabinet space, broom closet, chute for sweepings, and door to grade landing, leading to basement and outdoors. Three good size bedrooms are provided on second floor, each having large closets and connecting to center hall and bathroom. A brick water table extends around house, with wide lap siding above. Seven-foot basement under entire house, fitted with boiler, vegetable, laundry and recreation rooms.

15

Design No. 434

16

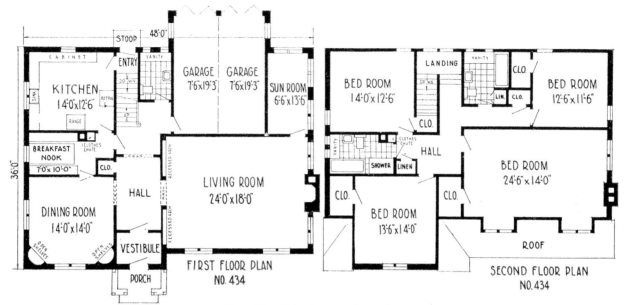

Plan No. 434—Size, 48 by 36 feet

This English type home with walls of brick slightly varied in color, natural wood trim, brown stained, neat appearing semi-recessed flat-roof dormers and artistic entrance porch is a decided departure in architectural design and extremely rich in appearance. Entrance is made through vestibule to center hall which has triple arched openings, to living room, dining room and rear hall with stairway, doors to kitchen and to double garage, and roomy lavatory with built-in vanity. The spacious living room is well lighted and has a fireplace. French door to sunroom, and recessed arches with open shelves for books and ornamental pieces. The dining room is extra large and has recessed corner arches with cabinet space below and open shelves above. The kitchen is good size and has cabinets along outside walls with sink and window openings in center, chimney for range, refrigerator space, breakfast room adjoining with clothes chute, and door to rear entry leading to basement and outdoors. The second floor arrangement is very compact and has four good size bedrooms, hall closet, linen closet, clothes chute and two bathrooms, each with built-in vanity with wall space for mirror between two casement windows. Seven-foot basement under entire house, with abundant space for extra large recreation room, lavatory, laundry, furnace, fruit, vegetable and storage rooms. Hot water heating plant with oil burner equipment is recommended. Air-conditioning equipment may be installed. Ceiling height, first floor, 8 feet 3 inches; second floor, 8 feet.

Design No. 435

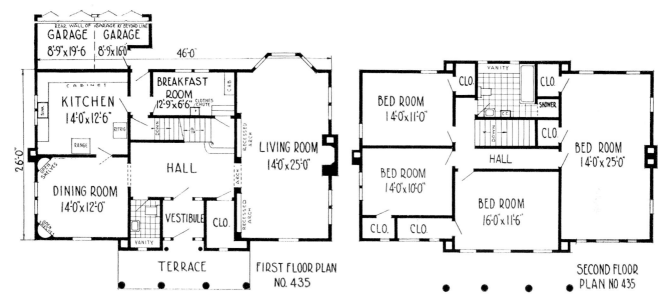

REAR WALL OF GARAGE 10' BEYOND LINE

GARAGE 8'-9"x19-6   GARAGE 8'-9"x16-0"

46-0"

26-0"

CABINET

KITCHEN 14'-0"x12'-6"

SINK

REFRIG

RANGE

OPEN SHELVES

DINING ROOM 14'-0"x12'-0"

BREAKFAST ROOM 12'-9"x6'-6"

CLOTHES CHUTE

CAB

DOWN

UP

HALL

RECESSED ARCH

LIVING ROOM 14'-0"x25'-0"

RECESSED ARCH

ARCH

RECESSED ARCH

VANITY

VESTIBULE

CLO.

TERRACE

FIRST FLOOR PLAN NO. 435

BED ROOM 14'-0"x11'-0"

CLO.

VANITY

CLO.

SHOWER

CLO.

BED ROOM 14'-0"x10'-0"

HALL

DOWN

CC

BED ROOM 14'-0"x25'-0"

CLO.

CLO.

BED ROOM 16'-0"x11'-6"

SECOND FLOOR PLAN NO 435

Plan No. 435—Size, 46 by 26 feet

This magnificent Southern-style Colonial home is truly the Home Beautiful. The columns in entrance way and supporting projected roof over terrace give this home a palatial and extra rich appearance. Entrance is made through vestibule to center hall, which has a lavatory, large coat closet, living room and dining room. The large living room is well lighted and has a fireplace, bay window at rear, and recessed arches with open shelves for books and ornamental pieces. The dining room is good size, and has recessed corner arches with cabinet space below and open or enclosed shelves above, and has swinging door to adjoining kitchen. The kitchen is very roomy and strictly modern, having cabinets entire length of two walls with sink and window opening in center, refrigerator space, chimney for range, and breakfast room adjoining with clothes chute, cabinet, and door to second floor stairway. The second floor arrangement includes a master bedroom and three other bedrooms, each having large closets, and a large bathroom with tub, shower, clothes chute and a built-in vanity with wall space for mirror between two casement windows. The exterior walls are of siding. Seven-foot basement under entire house with space for large recreation room, lavatory, laundry, furnace, vegetable, fruit and storage rooms. Hot water heating plant with oil burner equipment is recommended. Air-conditioning equipment may be installed. Ceiling height, first floor, 8 feet 3 inches; second floor, 8 feet.

Design No. 74

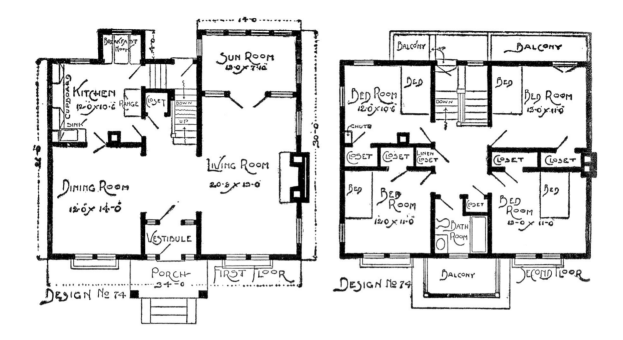

This attractive full two-story house is 34 feet in width by 26 feet in depth. The interior arrangement is very spacious and embodies all conveniences. The large center hall, having grand staircase, dining room on one side, with large living room on other side, having fireplace and French doors leading into sunroom, all combine in producing a thoroughly practical and strictly modern interior. The kitchen is provided with cupboard, chimney for range, breakfast nook, door leading to center hall, also door to grade landing, leading to basement and outdoors. There are four large roomy chambers on second floor, each having ample closet space, with access to center hall and bathroom. A linen closet, clothes chute, and rear balcony for airing bedding are included in the floor plan arrangement. A brick water table extends around house, with wide lap siding above. Basement under entire house, fitted with laundry tubs, storage room, vegetable cellar and dust-proof coal bin. Hot water heat recommended. Height of ceilings: First floor, 9 feet; second floor, 8 feet 3 inches.

Design No. 7

This magnificent English type home is 40 feet, 6 inches in width by 30 feet in depth, exclusive of sunroom projection. The double gable effect, stone trim entrance and attractive roof design, all combine in producing an exterior so much desired but seldom obtained in English type designing. The interior planning, with vestibule entrance and closet adjoining, reception hall with artistic plaster arch openings to living room, dining room and grand staircase, large living room with unique design fireplace, and French doors leading to porch and to sunroom, makes this a most palatial interior arrangement. The kitchen is very roomy and equipped with latest design fixtures and conveniences, and has a door to rear entry hall with broom closet adjoining. A toilet room is located between dining room and kitchen and may be utilized for breakfast room if so desired. The second floor arrangement includes three extra large chambers, each with roomy closets and connected with center hall. The bathroom is very good size, has tile floor and walls, up-to-date fixtures, including shower, towel cabinet, clothes locker and electric heater built in hall. The third floor arrangement provides for maids' room and bath, storage and cedar closets. Seven-foot basement extends under entire house, with large recreation room, boiler, laundry, preserve, storage and toilet rooms.

Design No. 421

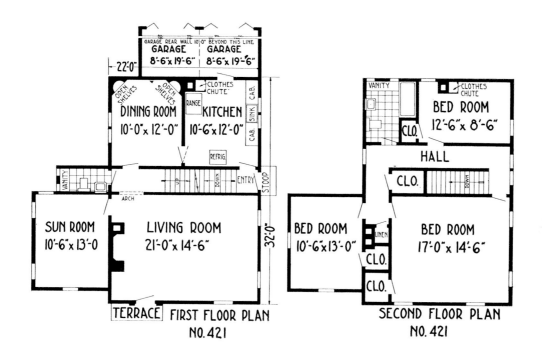

GARAGE REAR WALL 10'-0" BEYOND THIS LINE

GARAGE
8'-6"x 19'-6"

GARAGE
8'-6"x 19'-6"

22'-0"

OPEN SHELVES

OPEN SHELVES

CLOTHES CHUTE

RANGE

DINING ROOM
10'-0"x 12'-0"

KITCHEN
10'-6"x 12'-0"

CAB. SINK CAB.

REFRIG

VANITY

SUN ROOM
10'-6"x 13'-0

LIVING ROOM
21'-0"x 14'-6"

UP DOWN ENTRY

STOOP

32'-0"

ARCH

TERRACE FIRST FLOOR PLAN
NO. 421

VANITY

CLOTHES CHUTE

BED ROOM
12'-6"x 8'-6"

CLO.

HALL

CLO.

DOWN

BED ROOM
10'-6"x13'-0"

LINEN

CLO.

BED ROOM
17'-0"x 14'-6"

CLO.

SECOND FLOOR PLAN
NO. 421

Plan No. 421—Size, 22 by 32 feet

Plain lines and exterior walls of siding give this home a very cozy and inviting appearance. The large living room has a fireplace, French door to sunroom, arched opening to stairway hall with lavatory adjoining and French door to dining room. The kitchen has a cabinet with sink in center, chimney for range, clothes chute, refrigerator space, door to two-car garage in rear, and door to side entry leading to basement and outdoors. The second floor arrangement includes three bedrooms, clothes chute, hall closet and linen closet, and bathroom with built-in vanity with wall space for mirror between two casement windows. Seven-foot basement under entire house with space for recreation room, toilet, laundry, furnace, vegetable and storage rooms. Hot water heating plant with oil burner equipment is recommended. Air-conditioning equipment may be installed if desired. Ceiling height, first floor, 8 feet 3 inches; second floor, 8 feet.

25

Design No. 446

26

FIRST FLOOR PLAN
NO. 446

GARAGE 7'-6"x16'-0"
GARAGE 7'-6"x19'-6"
REAR WALL OF GARAGE IS BEYOND LINE
STOOP
ENTRY
RANGE
KITCHEN 10'-3"x10'-3"
DOWN
REFRIG.
CAB. SINK CAB.
UP
BREAKFAST NOOK
LIVING ROOM 13'-3"x28'-0"
RECESSED PORCH
CLOTHES CHUTE
PORCH 8'-0"x10'-0"
HALL
RECESSED ARCH
DINING ROOM 10'-3"x12'-0"
VEST. CLO.
SHELVES

SECOND FLOOR PLAN
NO. 446

BED ROOM 13'-3"x13'-0"
DOWN
BED ROOM 10'-6"x13'-0"
CLO. CLO. CLO.
HALL
CLO. CLO.
CLOTHES CHUTE
BED ROOM 13'-3"x12'-9"
SHOWER
VANITY
BED ROOM 10'-6"x13'-0"

Plan No. 446—Size, 32 by 30 feet

Combining stone and siding for front wall with upper portion projected over lower wall, artistic entrance design and side porch make a very effective and pleasing exterior design. Entry is made through vestibule to center hall, with coat closet, triple arched openings to living room, dining room and rear hall housing lavatory and stairway. The spacious living room is well lighted and has a fireplace and recessed arches with open shelves for books and ornamental pieces. The dining room has a recessed corner arch with cabinet space below and open or enclosed shelves above, and door to side porch. The kitchen has a cabinet with sink and window opening in center, chimney for range, refrigerator space, breakfast nook adjoining with clothes chute, and doors to two-car garage and to rear entry leading to basement and outdoors. The second floor arrangement includes four bedrooms, hall closet, clothes chute and bathroom with tub, shower and built-in vanity. The exterior is of siding except stone portion of front wall. Seven-foot basement under entire house with space for recreation room, toilet, laundry, furnace, vegetable and storage rooms. Hot water heating plant with oil burner equipment is recommended. Air-conditioning equipment optional. Ceiling height, first floor, 8 feet 3 inches; second floor, 8 feet.

Design No. 52

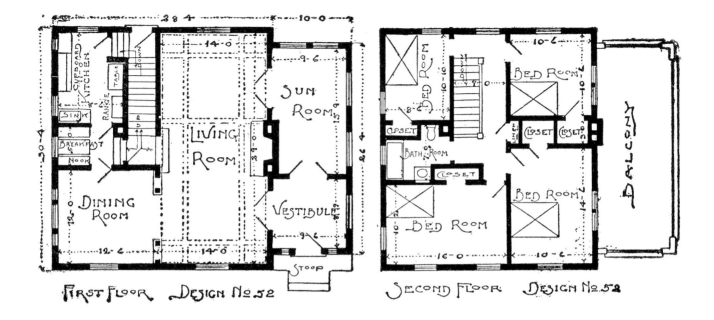

FIRST FLOOR · DESIGN Nº 52

SECOND FLOOR · DESIGN Nº 52

This exceptional attractive California style home is 28 feet 4 inches in width, by 30 feet 4 inches in depth, exclusive of vestibule and sunroom. The interior arrangement is very spacious and luxurious. The large living room with fireplace, having French doors on either side, leading to vestibule and to sunroom, and artistic bookcase arch leading into dining room, makes a perfect interior. A cozy breakfast nook is located between dining room and kitchen, with entrance to combination staircase, leading to second floor. The kitchen has a cupboard, chimney for range, and door to grade landing, leading to basement and outdoors. Four bedrooms are located on second floor, each having ample closet space and connected to small center hall and bathroom. Basement under entire house, fitted with laundry tubs, vegetable cellar, and dust-proof coal bin. Height of ceilings: First floor, 9 feet; second floor, 8 feet.

NOTE: Lumber, brick or a combination of both may be substituted in place of stucco.

Plan No. 405—Size, 34 by 30 feet

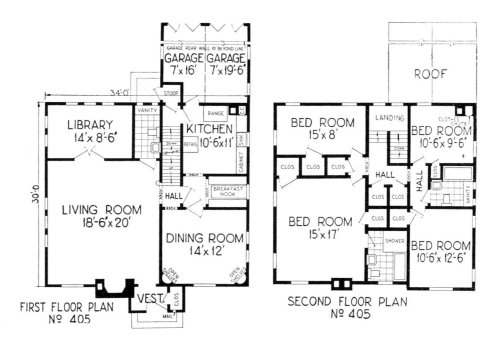

FIRST FLOOR PLAN
N⁰ 405

GARAGE 7'x16' | GARAGE 7'x19'-6'
GARAGE REAR WALL 10'BEYOND LINE
STOOP
VANITY
LIBRARY 14'x 8'-6'
KITCHEN 10'-6'x11'
RANGE
REFRIG
DOWN
UP
CABINET
SINK
HALL
BREAKFAST NOOK
LIVING ROOM 18'-6'x20'
DINING ROOM 14'x12'
OPEN SHELVES
OPEN SHELVES
VEST.
CLOS.
MAIL
34'-0
30'-0

SECOND FLOOR PLAN
N⁰ 405

ROOF
BED ROOM 15'x 8'
LANDING
CLOTHES CHUTE
BED ROOM 10'-6'x 9'-6'
CLOS. CLOS. CLOS.
HALL
HALL
CLOS.
CLOS. CLOS.
VANITY
DOWN
BED ROOM 15'x17'
CLOS. CLOS.
SHOWER
BED ROOM 10'-6'x 12'-6'

The projected brick wall vestibule and fireplace chimney and shingled walls produce a very pleasing and attractive exterior. Entrance is made through vestibule into large well-lighted living room having fireplace, French doors to library or sunroom, lavatory adjoining with built-in vanity, and arched entrance to stairway, and to dining room, which is concealed from view but may have an arched entrance in living room wall partition. The kitchen is provided with cabinet with sink in center, chimney for range, clothes chute, breakfast nook adjoining, door to double garage and door to rear entry leading to basement and outdoors. The second floor arrangement is ideal, with four bedrooms, two bathrooms, clothes chute and abundant closet space. The main bathroom has a built-in vanity and the private bathroom has a built-in shower. Maid's room and bathroom as well as additional closet and storage room may be provided on third floor. Exterior walls are covered with shingles except portion of front wall and vestibule of brick as shown in illustration. Seven-foot basement under entire house with ample space for recreation room, toilet room, laundry, furnace, vegetable and storage rooms. Hot water heating plant with oil burner equipment is recommended. Air-conditioning equipment may be installed. Ceiling height, first floor, 8 feet 3 inches; second floor, 8 feet.

Design No. 442

32

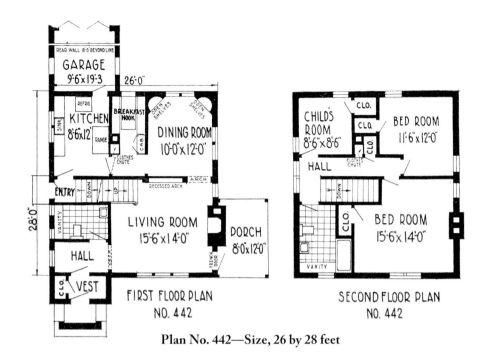

GARAGE
9'-6"x19-3

REAR WALL 10'-0" BEYOND LINE

26'-0"

REFRIG

KITCHEN
8'-6"x12'

BREAKFAST NOOK

SINK

RANGE

CAB.

OPEN SHELVES

OPEN SHELVES

DINING ROOM
10'-0"x12'-0"

CLOTHES CHUTE

ARCH.

RECESSED ARCH

ENTRY

DOWN

UP

28'-0"

VANITY

LIVING ROOM
15'-6"x14'-0"

PORCH
8'-0"x12'-0"

FRENCH DOOR

HALL

CLO.

VEST

FIRST FLOOR PLAN
NO. 442

CHILD'S ROOM
8'-6"x8'-6"

CLO.

CLO.

CLO.

HALL

CLOTHES CHUTE

BED ROOM
11'-6"x12'-0"

DOWN

CLO.

BED ROOM
15'-6"x14'-0"

VANITY

SECOND FLOOR PLAN
NO. 442

Plan No. 442—Size, 26 by 28 feet

The sloping gable roof extending over glazed porch, projected vestibule and walls of brick varied in color has made a very effective exterior design. The front vestibule has a coat closet and adjoins hall with lavatory and arched opening to cozy living room which has fireplace, French doors to side porch, arched opening to dining room and recessed arch with open shelves for books and ornamental pieces. The dining room has recessed corner arches with cabinet space below and open or enclosed shelves above. The kitchen has cabinet with sink and window opening in center, chimney for range, refrigerator space, breakfast nook adjoining with cabinet and clothes chute, door to garage and door to side entry leading to basement and outdoors. The second floor arrangement includes three bedrooms, hall closet, clothes chute and bathroom with built-in vanity and wall space for mirror between two casement windows. Seven-foot basement under entire house with space for recreation room, toilet, laundry, furnace, vegetable and storage rooms. Hot water heating plant with oil burner equipment is recommended. Air-conditioning equipment optional. Ceiling height, first floor, 8 feet 3 inches; second floor, 8 feet.

33

Design No. 431

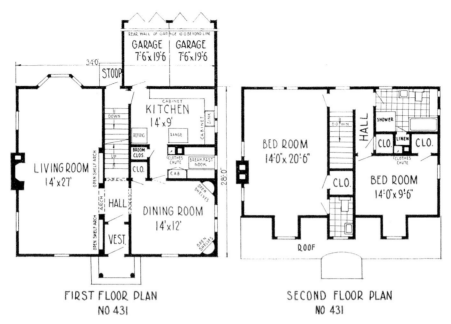

FIRST FLOOR PLAN
NO 431

SECOND FLOOR PLAN
NO 431

Plan No. 431—Size, 34 by 28 feet

The Colonial type semi-bungalow is always in favor and style. The extra wide windows with blinds and artistic triple dormers give the exterior broad, graceful lines. A brick water table extends around house with siding above. Entry is made through vestibule to center hall, which has triple arched openings to living room, dining room and stairway. The living room is exceptionally large and well lighted and has a fireplace, bay window at rear and recessed arches with open shelves for books and ornamental pieces. The dining room is good size and has recessed corner arches. The kitchen is well planned, having abundant cabinet space with sink and window openings in center, chimney for range, refrigerator space, breakfast nook adjoining with clothes chute, broom closet, and cabinet, door to two-car garage and door to rear entry leading to basement and outdoors. The second floor arrangement includes a master bedroom with lavatory adjoining, an extra bedroom, clothes chute, hall closet and large bathroom with tub, shower, linen closet and built-in vanity with wall space for mirror between two casement windows. Seven-foot basement under entire house with space for recreation room, toilet, laundry, furnace, vegetable and storage rooms. Type of heating plant with oil burner attachment is optional. Air-conditioning equipment may be installed. Ceiling height, first floor, 8 feet 3 inches; second floor, 8 feet.

Plan No. 408—Size, 26 by 36 feet plus 22 by 21 feet

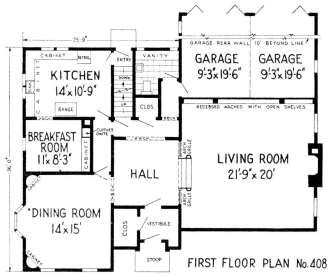

FIRST FLOOR PLAN No. 408

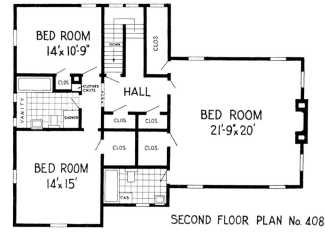

SECOND FLOOR PLAN No. 408

The gabled windows and projections, broad graceful lines and artistic entrance way produce a luxurious and palatial appearance. The house is 26 feet wide by 36 feet in depth excepting living room portion. The roomy vestibule with closet leads to center hall, which has arched opening to rear portion with coat closet, door to double garage, and to lavatory which has a built-in vanity with wall space for mirror between two casement windows, arch opening to dining room and triple arched opening to living room with grill rail in openings at side of center stair arch. The living room is spacious and well-lighted and has a fireplace and triple recessed arches in rear wall, with open shelves for ornamental pieces and books. The living room floor is two feet lower than floor in other portion of house and has stairs with wrought iron rails. The dining room is good size and has recessed corner arches with open shelves at top and cabinet below, all combining to make a gorgeous interior. The kitchen has cabinets along rear walls with sink and window openings in center, chimney for range, refrigerator space, large breakfast room adjoining with cabinet and clothes chute, and door to rear entry leading to basement and outdoors. The second floor arrangement includes three bedrooms and two bathrooms. The main bathroom has a shower and built-in vanity with wall space for mirror between two casement windows. The owner's room is extra large and well-lighted and has fireplace, separate bathroom adjoining and large closets. Two closets and clothes chute are located in hall. Seven-foot basement under entire house with ample space for large recreation room, toilet room, laundry, fruit, vegetable, furnace and storage rooms. Hot water heating plant with oil burner equipment is recommended. Air-conditioning equipment may be installed. Ceiling height, first floor, 8 feet 3 inches; second floor, 8 feet.

Plan No. 402—Size, 32 by 28 feet

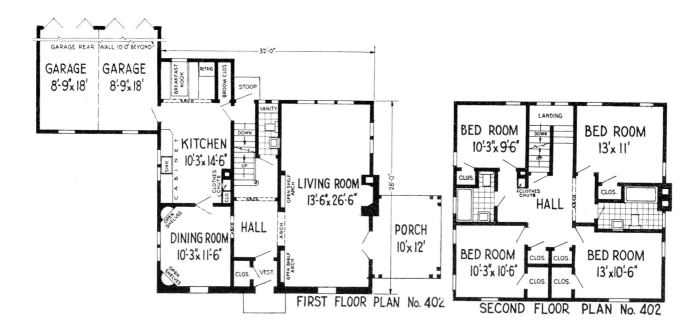

FIRST FLOOR PLAN No. 402

SECOND FLOOR PLAN No. 402

The combination of stone for lower portion of front wall with siding above, artistic window gables and entrance door design, the two-car garage at side with porch on other side giving the house broad lines, all contribute in producing this beautiful exterior design. The entire exterior is of siding except lower portion of front wall. The vestibule has a closet and adjoins center hall, which has arched openings to living room, dining room, stairway to second floor and lavatory with built-in vanity. The living room is good size and has fireplace, French doors to porch and recessed arches with open shelves for books and ornamental pieces. The dining room has recessed corner arches and swinging door to kitchen which is very modern, and includes cabinet with sink and window opening in center, chimney for range, clothes chute, breakfast nook, refrigerator space, broom closet, door to garage and door to rear entry leading to basement and outdoors. Seven-foot basement under entire house with space for large recreation room, toilet, laundry, furnace, fruit, vegetable and storage rooms. Hot water heating plant with oil burner equipment is recommended. Air-conditioning equipment may be installed if desired. Ceiling height, first floor, 8 feet 3 inches; second floor, 8 feet.

Design No. 426

40

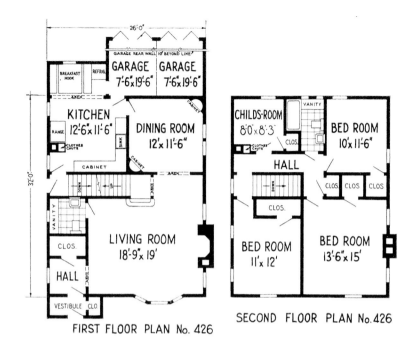

FIRST FLOOR PLAN No. 426

SECOND FLOOR PLAN No. 426

Plan No. 426—Size, 26 by 32 feet

An attractive home of siding with projected bay window and vestibule. The vestibule has a coat closet and adjoins hall with large closet and arched opening to spacious, well-lighted living room which has a fireplace, arched opening to dining room, stairway to second floor, and lavatory adjoining. The kitchen is very complete having cabinets along the inside walls with sink in center, chimney for range, clothes chute, breakfast nook adjoining with space for refrigerator and door to two-car garage, and door to side entry leading to basement and outdoors. The second floor arrangement includes three bedrooms and a child's room, clothes chute, hall closet and bathroom with built-in vanity and wall space for mirror between two casement windows. Seven-foot basement under entire house with space for recreation room, toilet, laundry, furnace, vegetable and storage rooms. Hot water heating plant with oil burner equipment is recommended. Air-conditioning equipment may be installed. Ceiling height, first floor, 8 feet 3 inches; second floor, 8 feet.

Design No. 432

42

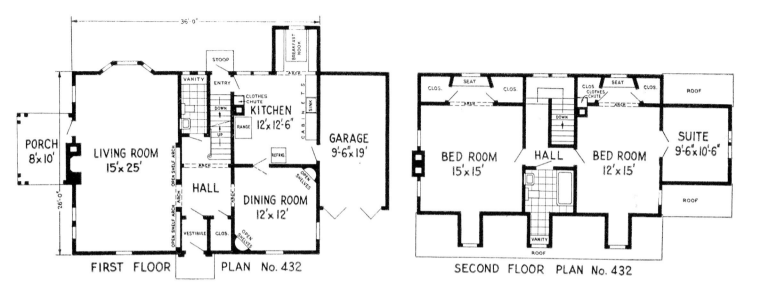

Plan No. 432—Size, 36 by 26 feet

A very attractive Colonial type semi-bungalow with porch and attached garage at either side. A brick water table extends around house with siding above. Entry is made through vestibule to center hall which has a coat closet, lavatory and triple arched openings to living room, dining room and to stairway. The living room is extra large and well lighted, having fireplace with French door at side to porch, and recessed corner arches. The kitchen is roomy and thoroughly modern, having cabinet with sink in center, chimney for range, clothes chute, refrigerator space, breakfast nook, door to garage and door to rear entry leading to basement and outdoors. The second floor arrangement includes two large bedrooms, one with French doors to adjoining lounge, clothes chute and bathroom with built-in vanity. Seven-foot basement under entire house with space for recreation room, toilet, laundry, furnace, vegetable and storage rooms. Type of heating plant with oil burner equipment is optional. Air-conditioning equipment may be installed. Ceiling height, first floor, 8 feet 3 inches; second floor, 8 feet.

Plan No. 414—Size, 26 by 34 feet

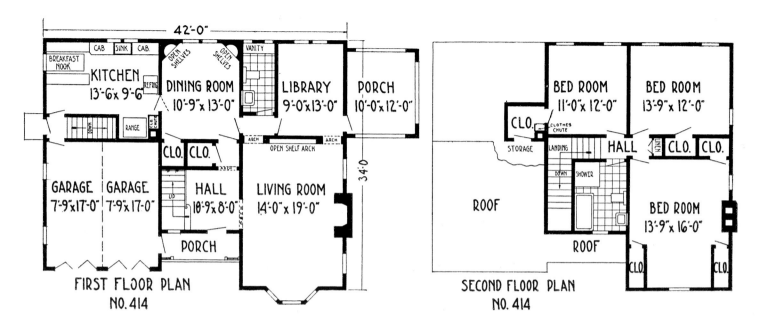

FIRST FLOOR PLAN NO. 414

42'-0"

BREAKFAST NOOK

CAB. | SINK | CAB.

KITCHEN 13'-6"x 9'-6"

REFRIG.

OPEN SHELVES

OPEN SHELVES

VANITY

DINING ROOM 10'-9"x 13'-0"

LIBRARY 9'-0"x13'-0"

PORCH 10'-0"x 12'-0"

RANGE

CLO. CHUTE

DOWN

34'-0"

CLO. | CLO.

ARCH

OPEN SHELF ARCH

ARCH

GARAGE 7'-9"x17'-0"

GARAGE 7'-9"x17'-0"

UP

HALL 10'-9"x 8'-0"

LIVING ROOM 14'-0"x 19'-0"

PORCH

SECOND FLOOR PLAN NO. 414

BED ROOM 11'-0"x 12'-0"

BED ROOM 13'-9"x 12'-0"

CLO.

CLOTHES CHUTE

STORAGE

LANDING

HALL

LINEN | CLO. | CLO.

DOWN | SHOWER

ROOF

BED ROOM 13'-9"x 16'-0"

ROOF

CLO.

CLO.

A modernistic type home with shingled exterior walls, double garage at one side and porch at other side is the very latest in popular design. The center hall has stairway to second floor, coat closet and arched opening to well-lighted living room which has a fireplace, bay window, recessed arch in rear wall with open shelves for ornamental pieces or books and arched openings at either side to library and to dining room and lavatory. The dining room is concealed from view of living room occupants affording a privacy so much desired, and has recessed corner arches with open shelves. The kitchen is very roomy and has a breakfast nook, cabinet with sink and window opening in center, chimney for range, clothes chute, refrigerator space, and door to rear entry leading to garage, to basement and outdoors. The second floor arrangement includes three bedrooms, clothes chute, linen closet and bathroom. Seven-foot basement under entire house with space for recreation room, toilet, laundry, furnace, vegetable and storage rooms. Hot water heating plant with oil burner equipment is recommended. Air-conditioning equipment may be installed. Ceiling height, first floor, 8 feet 3 inches; second floor, 8 feet.

Plan No. 404—Size, 22 by 30 feet plus 34 by 19 feet

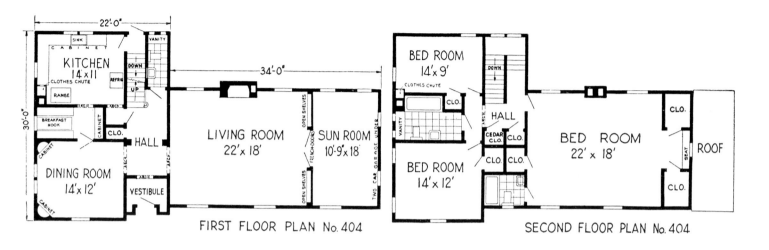

FIRST FLOOR PLAN No. 404

SECOND FLOOR PLAN No. 404

A home of distinction, stability and beauty with broad graceful lines, low roof construction sloping to first floor ceiling height over sunroom, artistic entrance way and conveniently located double garage under sunroom. The interior arrangement is thoroughly practical, convenient and ultra-modern. Entrance is made through vestibule to hall with arched openings to living room and dining room. The living room is spacious and well-lighted and has fireplace, French doors leading to sunroom and recessed arch at each side with open shelves for ornamental pieces or books. The dining room has recessed corner arches. The kitchen has cabinets along both outside walls with windows and sink in center, chimney for range, clothes chute, refrigerator space, breakfast nook adjoining with cabinet, and door to rear entry leading to basement and outdoors. The center hall has a lavatory with built-in vanity, and stairway to second floor where three bedrooms are provided. The large bedroom has bath adjoining, fireplace, window seat in dormer projection and ample closet space. The main bathroom has a built-in vanity. A cedar closet, clothes closet off center hall and clothes chute are also provided, all combining to produce a luxurious and palatial interior. A brick water table extends around entire house with siding above. Seven-foot basement under entire house with abundant space for large recreation room, laundry, furnace, fruit, vegetable and storage room, and toilet room. A hot water heating plant with oil burner equipment is recommended. Air-conditioning equipment may be installed. Ceiling height, first floor, 8 feet 3 inches; second floor, 8 feet.

Design No. 445

48

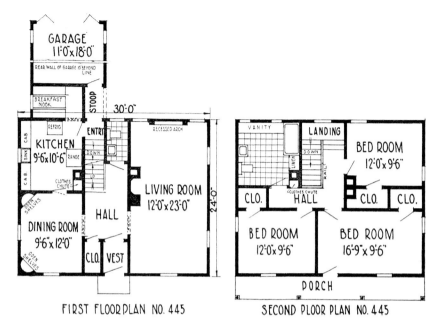

FIRST FLOOR PLAN NO. 445

SECOND FLOOR PLAN NO. 445

Plan No. 445—Size, 30 by 24 feet

A Southern Colonial type home with shingled walls, full-length blinds and bracketed porch across entire second floor front. Entrance is made through vestibule to center hall, which has a coat closet, lavatory and arched openings to living room and dining room. The large living room has a fireplace and recessed arch at rear with open shelves for books and ornamental pieces. The dining room has recessed corner arches with cabinet space below and open or enclosed shelves above. The kitchen is modern in every respect, having cabinet with sink and window opening in center, chimney for range, clothes chute, breakfast nook and door to rear entry leading to garage, basement and outdoors. The second floor arrangement includes three bedrooms, clothes closet and bathroom with linen closet and built-in vanity with wall space for mirror between two casement windows. Seven-foot basement under entire house with space for recreation room, toilet, laundry, furnace, vegetable and storage rooms. Hot water heating plant with oil burner equipment is recommended. Air-conditioning equipment optional. Ceiling height, first floor, 8 feet 3 inches; second floor, 8 feet.

49

Design No. 424

50

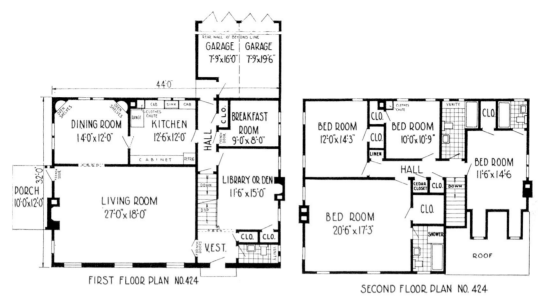

FIRST FLOOR PLAN NO. 424

SECOND FLOOR PLAN NO. 424

Plan No. 424—Size, 44 by 32 feet

The illustration best describes the beauty and palatial appearance of this distinctive type home. The exterior walls are covered with shingles except portion of front wall constructed of rock. Entrance is made through vestibule into spacious well-lighted living room which has a fireplace, French door to vestibule and to side porch, and arched opening to dining room. The vestibule has a lavatory adjoining, arched opening over stairway entrance and door leading to cozy library which has a fireplace, closet and door to rear hall. The kitchen is very modern and complete and has a cabinet with sink in center, chimney for range, clothes chute, refrigerator space and door to dining room and to rear hall with breakfast room adjoining, clothes closet, door to basement and to outdoors. The second floor arrangement includes four bedrooms, private bathroom adjoining master bedroom, linen closet, clothes chute, main bathroom with built-in vanity and lavatory adjoining bedroom over library. Seven-foot basement under entire house with ample space for large recreation room, toilet, laundry, furnace, vegetable, fruit and storage rooms. Hot water heating plant with oil burner equipment is recommended. Air-conditioning equipment may be installed if desired. Ceiling height, first floor, 8 feet 3 inches; second floor, 8 feet.

Plan No. 409—Size, 36 by 36 feet

52

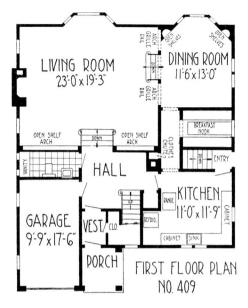

LIVING ROOM
23'-0" x 19'-3"

DINING ROOM
11'-6" x 13'-0"

OPEN SHELVES

OPEN SHELVES

ARCH GRILLE RAIL

DOWN

ARCH GRILLE RAIL

OPEN SHELF ARCH

DOWN

OPEN SHELF ARCH

BREAKFAST NOOK

CLOTHES CHUTE

HALL

VANITY

DOWN

ENTRY

KITCHEN
11'-0" x 11'-9"

RANGE

REFRIG.

CABINET

GARAGE
9'-9" x 17'-6"

VEST.

CLO.

CABINET

SINK

PORCH

FIRST FLOOR PLAN
NO. 409

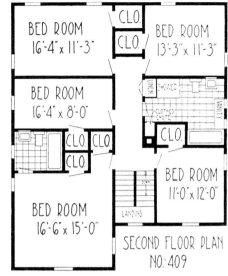

BED ROOM
16'-4" x 11'-3"

CLO.

CLO.

BED ROOM
13'-3" x 11'-3"

BED ROOM
16'-4" x 8'-0"

LINEN

SHOWER

CLOTHES CHUTE

VANITY

CLO.

CLO.

CLO.

BED ROOM
11'-0" x 12'-0"

BED ROOM
16'-6" x 15'-0"

DOWN

LANDING

SECOND FLOOR PLAN
NO. 409

This Modernistic type home with shingled exterior walls, front garage and kitchen and arched recessed entrance way is very unique and beautiful and the most popular design to be created. Entrance is made through vestibule to center hall which has stairway to second floor, coat closet, lavatory adjoining, with built-in vanity, and stairs with wrought iron rails leading to living room, the floor of which is two feet lower than floor of other portion of house. The living room is very spacious and exceptionally well-lighted and has fireplace, recessed arched opening at either side of stairway, with open shelves for ornamental pieces and books, bay window at rear and staircase leading to dining room and triple arched openings in partition wall with grill rail in openings each side of stairway, all combining to produce a luxurious interior. The dining room has bay windows at rear and recessed corner arches.

The kitchen has cabinets along outside walls with sink and window openings in center, refrigerator space, chimney for range, clothes chute, breakfast nook adjoining, and door to front hall and to rear entry leading to basement and outdoors. The second floor arrangement includes five bedrooms, two bathrooms, clothes chute, closet and linen closet. The owner's bedroom has a separate bathroom and the main bathroom has a shower, and built-in vanity with wall space for mirror between two casement windows. Seven-foot basement under entire house with ample space for large recreation room, toilet room, laundry, furnace, fruit, vegetable and storage rooms. Hot water heating plant with oil burner equipment is recommended. Air-conditioning equipment may be installed. Ceiling height, first floor, 8 feet 3 inches; second floor, 8 feet.

Plan No. 416—Size, 34 by 30 feet

54

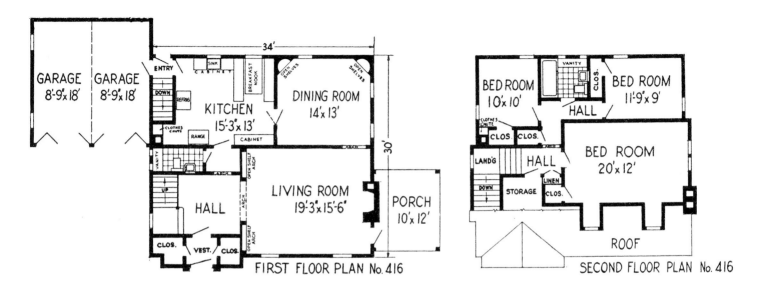

GARAGE 8'-9"x18'

GARAGE 8'-9"x18'

ENTRY

SINK CABINET

DOWN

BREAKFAST NOOK

REFRIG

KITCHEN 15'-3"x13'

CLOTHES CHUTE

RANGE

CABINET

VANITY

OPEN SHELF ARCH

UP

HALL

ARCH

OPEN SHELF ARCH

CLOS.

VEST.

CLOS.

34'

OPEN SHELVES

DINING ROOM 14'x13'

OPEN SHELVES

30'

ARCH

LIVING ROOM 19'-3"x15'-6"

PORCH 10'x12'

FIRST FLOOR PLAN No. 416

BED ROOM 10'x10'

VANITY

CLOS.

BED ROOM 11'-9"x9'

HALL

CLOTHES CHUTE

CLOS.

CLOS.

LAND'G

DOWN

HALL

STORAGE

LINEN

CLOS.

BED ROOM 20'x12'

ROOF

SECOND FLOOR PLAN No. 416

The bungalow roof with artistic dormers, double garage at one side and porch at other side produces a very pleasing and cozy exterior and is a very popular design that will stay in style for many years to come. Entry is made through front vestibule, with closets at each side, to hall, which has lavatory adjoining, and arched opening into well-lighted and roomy living room with fireplace, French door to porch, recessed arches in side wall with open shelves for ornamental pieces or books, and arched opening to dining room, which has recessed corner arches with open shelves. The kitchen is ample size and has a cabinet with sink and window opening in center, chimney for range, clothes chute, refrigerator space, breakfast nook, and door to rear entry leading to double garage, to basement and outdoors. The second floor arrangement includes three bedrooms, hall closet, linen closet, clothes chute, and bathroom with built-in vanity with wall space for mirror between two casement windows. A brick water table extends around house with siding above. Seven-foot basement under entire house with space for recreation room, toilet, laundry, furnace, vegetable and storage rooms. Hot water heating plant with oil burner equipment is recommended. Air-conditioning equipment may be installed. Ceiling height, first floor, 8 feet 3 inches; second floor, 8 feet.

Design No. 440

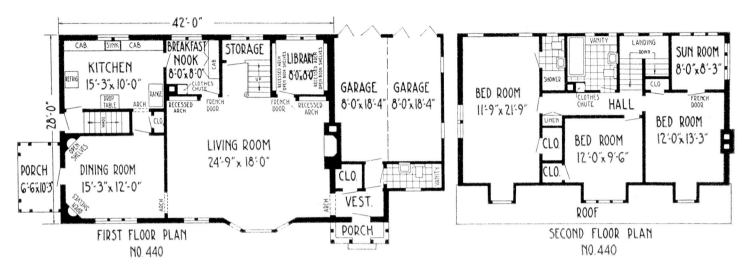

FIRST FLOOR PLAN
NO. 440

SECOND FLOOR PLAN
NO. 440

Plan No. 440—Size, 42 by 28 feet

An English type home with broad front, bungalow roof lines, walls of brick varied in color, natural wood trim stained brown, mission type entrance design all combine to produce this magnificent exterior design. The vestibule entrance has a coat closet, door to two-car garage, door to lavatory with built-in vanity, and arched opening to spacious and luxurious living room which has a fireplace, center staircase with storage space under landing, arched opening to dining room, French doors to library and breakfast room at either side of staircase, and recessed arches at each side of rear wall with open shelves for ornamental pieces. The dining room has doors to side porch and to kitchen entry, and recessed corner arches with cabinet space below and open or enclosed shelves above. The kitchen is completely modern, having cabinet with sink and window opening in center, refrigerator space, chimney for range, drop table, breakfast room adjoining with cabinet and clothes chute and door to side entry leading to basement and outdoors. The second floor arrangement includes three bedrooms with sunroom adjoining one room and lavatory with shower adjoining owner's room. Linen closet, clothes chute and bathroom with built-in vanity with wall space for mirror between two casement windows are also provided for. Seven-foot basement under entire house with abundant space for large recreation room, lavatory, laundry, furnace, fruit, vegetable and storage rooms. Hot water heating plant with oil burner equipment is recommended. Air-conditioning equipment optional. Ceiling height, first floor, 8 feet 3 inches; second floor, 8 feet.

Design No. 430

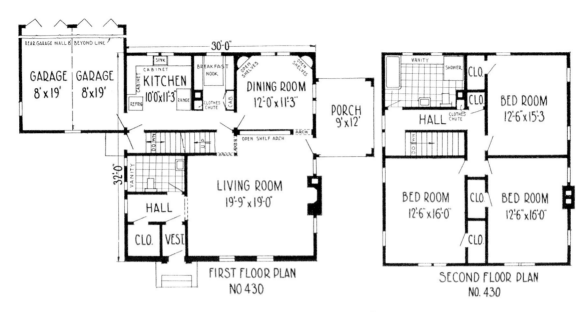

Plan No. 430—Size, 30 by 32 feet

An exceptionally attractive home with exterior walls of siding combined with stone for lower portion of front wall and fireplace chimney. Entrance is made through vestibule to hall, with large coat closet, lavatory adjoining, and arched opening to spacious well-lighted living room, which has a fireplace, French door to side porch, arched openings to stairway and to dining room, and recessed arch with open shelves for books or ornamental pieces. The dining room has recessed corner arches with open shelves in top portion and cabinet space below. The kitchen has cabinets along two walls with sink and window openings in center and refrigerator space at end, breakfast nook adjoining with cabinet, clothes chute, and door to dining room, doors to two-car garage and to side entry leading to basement and outdoors. The second floor arrangement includes three large bedrooms, clothes chute, hall closet, and large bathroom having tub, shower and built-in vanity with wall space for mirror between two casement windows. Seven-foot basement under entire house with ample space for large recreation room, toilet, laundry, furnace, fruit, vegetable and storage rooms. Hot water heating plant with oil burner equipment is recommended. Air-conditioning equipment may be installed. Ceiling height, first floor, 8 feet 3 inches; second floor, 8 feet.

Plan No. 407—Size, 30 by 30 feet

60

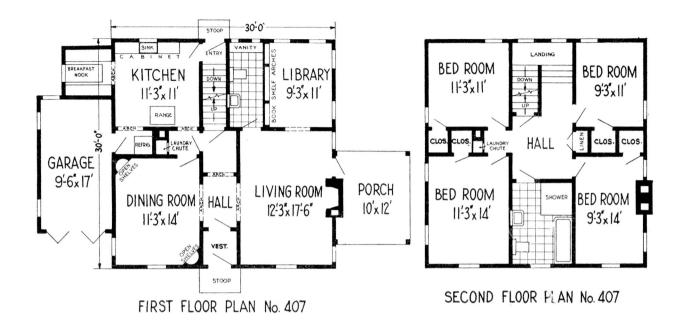

FIRST FLOOR PLAN No. 407

SECOND FLOOR PLAN No. 407

The Colonial type home is always popular and the design illustrated above with garage and porch at either side, is very attractive and stately. A brick water table extends around house with siding above. The interior arrangement is very compact and convenient. The living room has a fireplace with door at side leading to porch, and arched entrance to library with triple recessed arches with open shelves for books. A lavatory with built-in vanity adjoins. The dining room has recessed corner arches. The passage-way space between dining room and kitchen has a chimney for kitchen range, clothes chute, refrigerator space and door to garage. The

kitchen has a cabinet with sink in center, breakfast nook adjoining, and door to rear entry leading to basement and outdoors. Four bedrooms are located on second floor as well as bathroom. A linen closet and clothes chute are located in hall, also stairway to third floor where space is available for maid's quarters, additional closets and storage space. Seven-foot basement under entire house with space for recreation room, toilet, laundry, furnace, vegetable and storage rooms. Hot water heating plant with oil burner equipment is recommended. Air-conditioning equipment may be installed. Ceiling height, first floor, 8 feet 3 inches; second floor, 8 feet.

Plan No. 410—Size, 36 by 30 feet

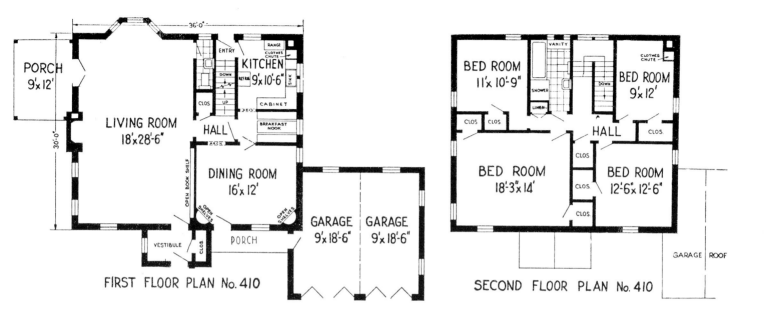

PORCH
9'x 12'

30'-0"

36'-0"

ENTRY

KITCHEN
9'x 10'-6"

RANGE

CLOTHES CHUTE

DOWN

REFRIG.

SINK

LIVING ROOM
18'x 28'-6"

CLOS.

UP

CABINET

HALL

BREAKFAST NOOK

OPEN BOOK SHELF

DINING ROOM
16'x 12'

OPEN SHELVES

OPEN SHELVES

PORCH

GARAGE
9'x 18'-6"

GARAGE
9'x 18'-6"

VESTIBULE

CLOS.

FIRST FLOOR PLAN No. 410

VANITY

SHOWER

CLOTHES CHUTE

LINEN

DOWN

BED ROOM
11'x 10'-9"

BED ROOM
9'x 12'

CLOS.

CLOS.

CLOS.

HALL

CLOS.

BED ROOM
18'-3"x 14'

CLOS.

BED ROOM
12'-6"x 12'-6"

CLOS.

GARAGE ROOF

SECOND FLOOR PLAN No. 410

With exterior walls of buff-color brick, projected vestibule, porch and double garage, the exterior design is unique, very luxurious and commanding in appearance. The large vestibule with coat closet leads to spacious and well-lighted living room which has a fireplace, French doors to side porch, recessed arched opening in side wall with open shelves for ornamental pieces or books, lavatory adjoining, and arched openings to small center hall which has a closet, stairway to second floor and connects all first floor rooms. The dining room has recessed corner arches and the kitchen has a cabinet with sink and window opening in center, clothes chute, chimney for range, refrigerator space, breakfast nook adjoining,

and door to rear entry leading to basement and outdoors. The second floor arrangement includes four bedrooms, each with ample size closets, hall closet and linen closet, and bathroom with shower and built-in vanity with wall space for mirror between two casement windows. Seven-foot basement under entire house with ample space for large recreation room, laundry, furnace, vegetable, fruit, storage and toilet rooms. Hot water heating plant with oil burner equipment is recommended. Air-conditioning equipment may be installed. Ceiling height, first floor, 8 feet 3 inches; second floor, 8 feet.

Design No. 437

64

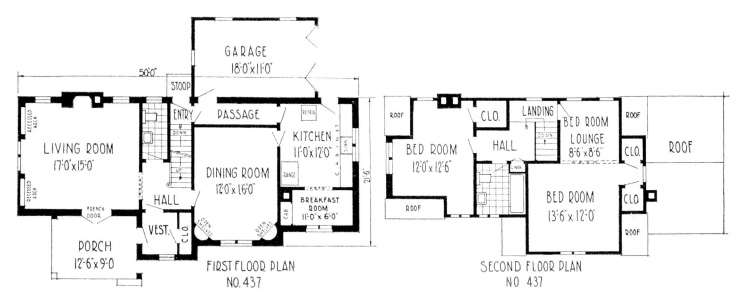

Plan No. 437—Size, 50 feet by 21 feet 6 inches

This attractive semi-bungalow borrows from the English type, with varied color brick for exterior walls and stained natural wood trim. An ideal design for a corner lot, with living room, dining room and kitchen having front exposure. Entrance is made through vestibule to hall which has a coat closet, stairway to second floor, lavatory and arched openings to living room and dining room. The living room has a fireplace, French doors to front porch and recessed arches with open shelves for books and ornamental pieces. The dining room being completely concealed affords privacy so much desired and has recessed corner arches with cabinet space below and open or enclosed shelves above. The kitchen is roomy and has a cabinet with sink and window opening in center, chimney for range, refrigerator space, breakfast nook with cabinet, and door to rear entry leading to garage, to basement and outdoors. The second floor takes in entire house area except portion over kitchen and the arrangement includes owner's suite and extra bedroom, linen closet and bathroom. Seven-foot basement under entire house with space for recreation room, toilet, laundry, furnace, vegetable and storage rooms. Hot water heating plant with oil burner equipment is recommended. Air-conditioning equipment may be installed. Ceiling height, first floor, 8 feet 3 inches; second floor, 8 feet.

Design No. 427

66

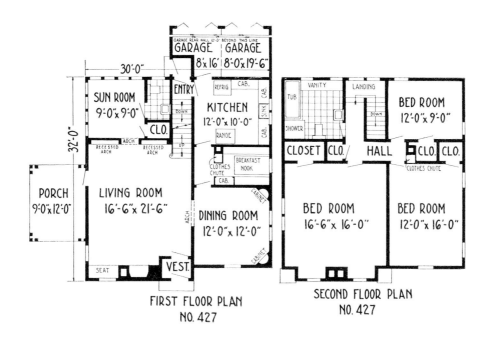

Plan No. 427—Size, 30 by 32 feet

A very cozy and unique design with front fireplace and shingled walls. Entrance is made through vestibule into large and well-lighted living room having fireplace, French door to side porch and to sunroom with recessed arches on either side with open shelves for books and ornamental pieces, stairway to second floor and arched opening to dining room, which has recessed corner arches. The sunroom has a coat closet and lavatory adjoining. The kitchen has cabinet along two walls with refrigerator space at one end and sink and window opening in center, chimney for range, door to two-car garage, breakfast nook adjoining with cabinet and clothes chute, and door to rear entry leading to basement and outdoors. The second floor arrangement includes three bedrooms, clothes chute, hall closet, stairway to attic, and roomy bathroom with shower, tub, and built-in vanity with wall space for mirror between two casement windows. Seven-foot basement under entire house with ample space for large recreation room, toilet, laundry, furnace, vegetable and storage rooms. Ceiling height, first floor, 8 feet 3 inches; second floor, 8 feet.

Plan No. 401—Size, 36 by 26 feet

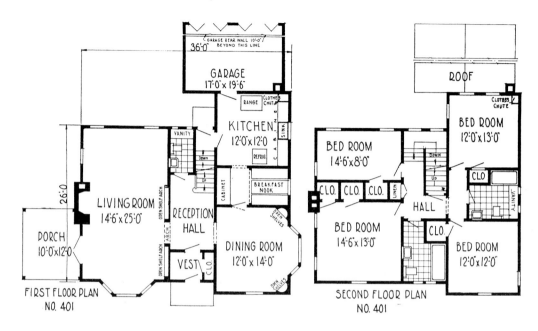

GARAGE REAR WALL 10'0"
BEYOND THIS LINE

36'0"

GARAGE
17'0" x 19'6"

RANGE   CLOTHES CHUTE

KITCHEN
12'0" x 12'0"

REFRIG

SINK
CAB.

VANITY

DOWN

UP

CABINET

BREAKFAST
NOOK

26'0"

LIVING ROOM
14'6" x 25'0"

RECEPTION
HALL

OPEN SHELF ARCH

OPEN SHELF ARCH

PORCH
10'0" x 12'0"

VEST.

CLO.

DINING ROOM
12'0" x 14'0"

OPEN SHELVES

OPEN SHELVES

FIRST FLOOR PLAN
NO. 401

ROOF

CLOTHES
CHUTE

BED ROOM
12'0" x 13'0"

CLO.

BED ROOM
14'6" x 8'0"

CLO.   CLO.   CLO.   LINEN

DOWN

UP

HALL

VANITY

BED ROOM
14'6" x 13'0"

CLO.

BED ROOM
12'0" x 12'0"

SECOND FLOOR PLAN
NO. 401

A strictly modern design that will always remain in style. The exterior effect is very pleasing and attractive. A brick water table extends around house with siding above. Entry is made through vestibule to center hall, which has arched openings to living room and dining room, stairway to second floor and lavatory at rear with built-in vanity. The living room is spacious and well-lighted and has fireplace, French doors to side porch and recessed arches with open shelves for books and ornamental pieces. The kitchen has a cabinet with sink and window opening in center, chimney for range, clothes chute, refrigerator space, breakfast room adjoining with separate cabinet, door to two-car garage and door to rear entry leading to basement and outdoors. The second floor arrangement includes four bedrooms, two bathrooms, one with built-in vanity with wall space for mirror between two casement windows, linen closet, and clothes chute. Seven-foot basement under entire house with ample space for large recreation room, toilet, laundry, furnace, fruit, vegetable and storage rooms. Hot water heating plant with oil burner equipment is recommended. Air-conditioning equipment may be installed if desired. Ceiling height, first floor, 8 feet 3 inches; second floor, 8 feet.

Plan No. 413—Size, 34 by 28 feet

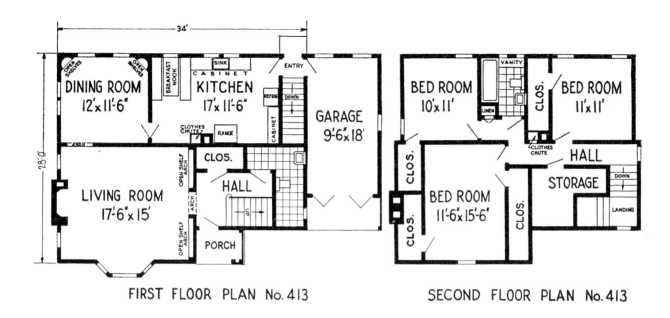

FIRST FLOOR PLAN No. 413

SECOND FLOOR PLAN No. 413

This Modernistic design home with attached garage at side, bay window and semi-bungalow roof construction has extremely graceful lines and a luxurious appearance. The front entrance hall has a lavatory under stairway to second floor, large clothes closet and arched entrance to attractive living room which has a fireplace, recessed arched openings with open shelves for ornamental pieces or books and arched opening to dining room which has recessed corner arches. The kitchen is very roomy and has a cabinet with sink and window openings along outside wall, another cabinet with refrigerator space, clothes chute, chimney for range, breakfast nook, and door to rear entry leading to garage, to basement and outdoors. The second floor arrangement includes three bedrooms, clothes chute, linen closet and bathroom with built-in vanity with wall space for mirror between two casement windows. Seven-foot basement under entire house with space for recreation room, toilet, laundry, furnace, vegetable and storage rooms. Hot water heating plant with oil burner equipment is recommended. Air-conditioning equipment may be installed. Ceiling height, first floor, 8 feet 3 inches; second floor, 8 feet.

71

Design No. 429

72

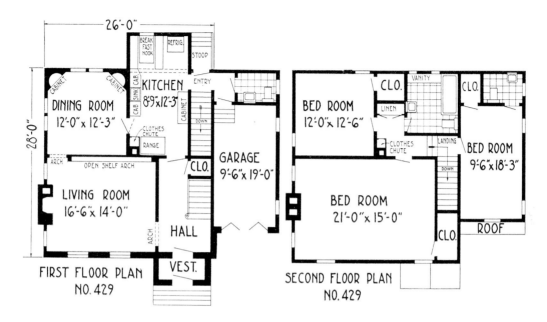

Plan No. 429—Size, 26 by 28 feet

Using stone for lower portion of front wall and siding above produces an artistic exterior. A roomy vestibule adjoins front hall and has coat closet, stairway to second floor, door to kitchen and arched opening to attractive, well-lighted living room, which has a fireplace, arched opening to dining room and recessed arch with open shelves for books and ornamental pieces. The dining room has recessed corner arches with open shelves in top portion and cabinet space below. The kitchen is conveniently arranged with cabinet with sink in center, chimney for range, breakfast nook, refrigerator space, and rear entry adjoining with lavatory, and doors to garage, basement stairway and outdoors. The second floor arrangement includes three bedrooms, lavatory adjoining one room, clothes chute, linen closet and roomy bathroom with built-in vanity and wall space for mirror between two casement windows. Exterior walls are of siding except stone portion of front wall. Seven-foot basement under entire house with space for recreation room, toilet, laundry, furnace, vegetable and storage rooms. Hot water heating plant with oil burner equipment is recommended. Air-conditioning equipment may be installed. Ceiling height, first floor, 8 feet 3 inches; second floor, 8 feet.

Design No. 436

74

Plan No. 436—Size, 38 by 22 feet

Combining common brick, painted white, with wide siding for portion of front wall and fireplace chimney, projecting main portion of living room beyond main body of house and providing wide gables over second floor windows has produced a distinctive type and exceptionally attractive exterior. The entrance hall has an open staircase with wrought iron grille rail, coat closet, lavatory, arched opening to living room and door to kitchen. The spacious well-lighted living room has a fireplace, bay windows at front and recessed arches across rear wall with open shelves for books and ornamental pieces and opening in center to dining room. The dining room has recessed corner arches with cabinet space below and open or enclosed shelves at top, and door to rear entry connecting with kitchen. The kitchen is thoroughly modern and roomy, hav-ing cabinet with sink and window openings in center, chimney for range, clothes chute, broom closet, refrigerator space, drop table and breakfast nook, door to two-car garage and door to rear entry leading to basement and outdoors. The second floor arrangement includes four good size bedrooms, clothes chute, linen closet and bathroom with tub, shower and built-in vanity with wall space for mirror between two casement windows. Seven-foot basement under entire house with abundant space for large recreation room, lavatory, laundry, furnace, fruit, vegetable and storage rooms. Hot water heating plant with oil burner equipment is recommended. Air-conditioning equipment may be installed. Ceiling height, first floor, 8 feet 3 inches; second floor, 8 feet.

Plan No. 411—Size, 36 by 34 feet

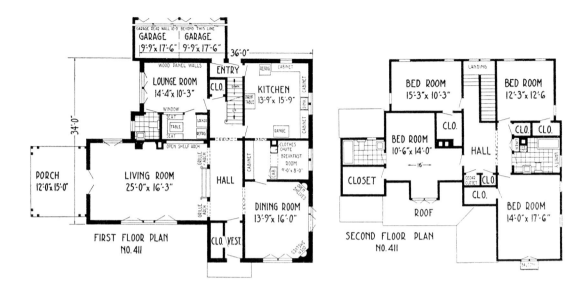

GARAGE DEAD WALL 10'-0" BEYOND THIS LINE

GARAGE
9'-9" x 17'-6"

GARAGE
9'-9" x 17'-6"

36'-0"

WOOD PANEL WALLS

ENTRY

REFRIG. CABINET

LOUNGE ROOM
14'-4" x 10'-3"

CLO.

KITCHEN
13'-9" x 15'-9"

DROP TABLE

CABINET

SINK

WINDOW SEAT
TABLE
SEAT

LOCKER
REFRIG.

RANGE

CABINET

34'-0"

OPEN SHELF ARCH

CLOTHES CHUTE

GRILLE ARCH

CABINET

BREAKFAST ROOM
9'-0" x 8'-0"

CAB.

PORCH
12'-0" x 15'-0"

LIVING ROOM
25'-0" x 16'-3"

HALL

GRILLE ARCH

OPEN SHELVES

FIRST FLOOR PLAN
NO. 411

CLO. VEST.

DINING ROOM
13'-9" x 16'-0"

LANDING

BED ROOM
15'-3" x 10'-3"

BED ROOM
12'-3" x 12'-6

CLO.

BED ROOM
10'-6" x 14'-0"

CLO. CLO.

HALL

CLOSET

16

VANITY

CEDAR CLOSET
CLO.

CLO.

ROOF

BED ROOM
14'-0" x 17'-6"

SECOND FLOOR PLAN
NO. 411

A truly English type home with exterior walls of buff-color brick, stained wood trim, casement windows, broad front partly projected with graceful sloping roof construction is a unique design and extremely attractive. Entry through vestibule to center hall which has an arched opening to rear portion which contains stairway to second floor, clothes closet, and French doors to lounge room which has wood panel walls, lavatory, service nook with table and seats, refrigerator space and locker closet. The living room is very spacious and well lighted and has fireplace, French doors to porch, recessed arch in portion of rear wall with open shelves for ornamental pieces or books. The living room floor is two feet below floor level of other portion of house and has a triple arch opening to hall with wrought iron rail in openings at either side of stairway arch. The dining room has an arched opening to hall, also recessed corner arches with open shelves, all combining to produce a very luxurious interior. The kitchen has cabinets along outside walls with sink and window openings in center and refrigerator built in at one end, chimney for range, breakfast room adjoining with cabinets and clothes chute, door to center hall, and door to rear entry leading to double garage, to basement and outdoors. The second floor arrangement is very complete, four good size bedrooms, plenty of closets, clothes chute, linen closet and two bathrooms. The owner's room has separate bathroom and the main bathroom has a shower and built-in vanity with wall space for mirror between two casement windows. Seven-foot basement under entire house with abundant space for large recreation room, toilet room, laundry, furnace, fruit, vegetable and storage rooms. Hot water heating plant with oil burner equipment is recommended. Air-conditioning equipment may be installed. Ceiling height, first floor, 8 feet 3 inches; second floor, 8 feet.

Plan No. 403—Size, 32 by 28 feet

78

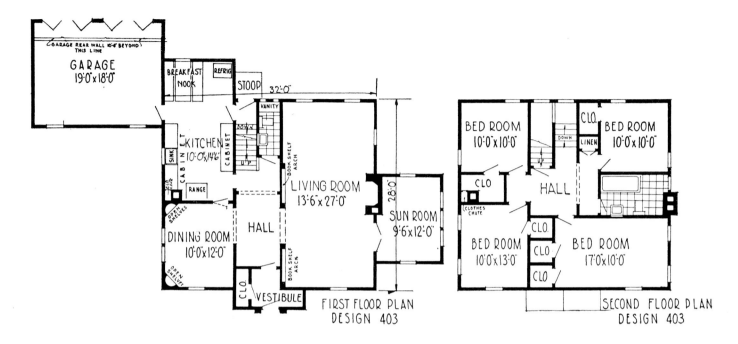

GARAGE 19'-0" x 18'-0"

GARAGE REAR WALL 10'-0" BEYOND THIS LINE

BREAKFAST NOOK

REFRIG

STOOP

32'-0"

VANITY

KITCHEN 10'-0" x 14'-6"

CABINET

CABINET

SINK

UP

RANGE

OPEN SHELVES

BOOK SHELF ARCH

LIVING ROOM 13'-6" x 27'-0"

28'-0"

SUN ROOM 9'-6" x 12'-0"

DINING ROOM 10'-0" x 12'-0"

HALL

OPEN SHELVES

BOOK SHELF ARCH

CLO

VESTIBULE

FIRST FLOOR PLAN DESIGN 403

BED ROOM 10'-0" x 10'-0"

CLO.

BED ROOM 10'-0" x 10'-0"

DOWN

LINEN

CLO

HALL

UP

CLOTHES CHUTE

CLO.

BED ROOM 10'-0" x 13'-0"

CLO

CLO

BED ROOM 17'-0" x 10'-0"

CLO

SECOND FLOOR PLAN DESIGN 403

The gables over windows and vestibule projection, shingled walls and garage and sunroom at either side give this house a warm rich appearance. Entry is made through roomy vestibule to center hall which has triple arched openings to living room, dining room and rear hall enclosing stairway and lavatory. The large living room is well-lighted and has a fireplace, French doors to sunroom and recessed arches with open shelves for books and ornamental pieces. The dining room has recessed corner arches and swinging door to kitchen which has a cabinet with sink and window opening in center, chimney for range, clothes chute, breakfast nook, refrigerator space, door to garage and door to rear entry leading to basement and outdoors. The second floor arrangement includes four bedrooms, bathroom with built-in vanity and wall space for mirror between two casement windows, clothes chute and linen closet. Seven-foot basement under entire house with ample space for recreation room, toilet, laundry, furnace, fruit, vegetable and storage rooms. Hot water heating plant with oil burner equipment is recommended. Air-conditioning equipment may be installed if desired. Ceiling height, first floor, 8 feet 3 inches; second floor, 8 feet.

Design No. 423

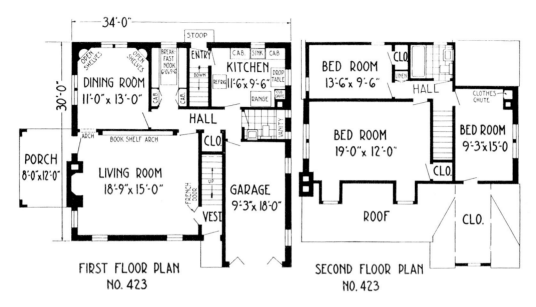

Plan No. 423—Size, 34 by 30 feet

Borrowing from the Cape Cod style this attractive semi-bungalow has a rich and pleasing exterior with front garage and porch at side. Entrance is made through vestibule into large well-lighted living room which has a fireplace, French door to vestibule, and recessed arch along rear wall with open shelves for books or ornamental pieces, with arched opening at one side to dining room and arched door at other side to center hall. The dining room has corner recessed arches and has double windows in outside walls. The kitchen has a cabinet with sink in center, chimney for range, clothes chute, refrigerator space, door to hall leading to garage, lavatory, breakfast nook with cabinets, and dining room. A door to rear entry is also provided leading to basement and outdoors. The exterior walls are brick-veneered. The second floor arrangement includes three bedrooms, clothes chute, linen closet, and bathroom with a built-in vanity with wall space for mirror between two casement windows. Seven-foot basement under entire house with space for recreation room, toilet, furnace, laundry, vegetable and storage rooms. Hot water heating plant with oil burner equipment is recommended. Air-conditioning equipment may be installed if desired. Ceiling height, first floor, 8 feet 3 inches; second floor, 8 feet.

Design No. 441

82

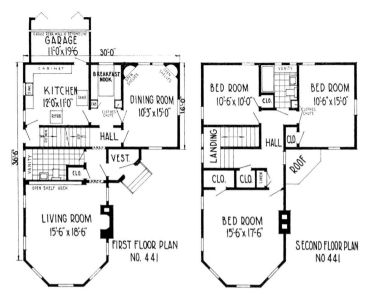

Plan No. 441—Size, 30 by 26 feet (average)

Projecting entire living room portion beyond main body of house and providing corner vestibule entrance has produced a design individual in type and attractiveness. The vestibule entrance leads to hall with double arched openings to living room and stairway, lavatory with built-in vanity, French door to dining room and door to kitchen. The spacious living room is exceptionally well lighted and has a fireplace and recessed arch with open shelves for books and ornamental pieces. The dining room is completely concealed from living room affording a privacy very much desired and has recessed corner arches with cabinet space below and open or enclosed shelves above. The kitchen is roomy and strictly modern, having cabinets with sink and window opening in center of one,

chimney for range, refrigerator space, breakfast room adjoining with clothes chute, door to garage and door to side entry leading to basement and outdoors. The second floor arrangement includes three bedrooms, hall closet, linen closet, clothes chute and bathroom with built-in vanity with wall space for mirror between two casement windows. A brick water table extends around house with siding above. Seven-foot basement under entire house with ample space for large recreation room and fireplace under living room, also toilet, laundry, furnace, vegetable and storage rooms. Hot water heating plant with oil burner equipment is recommended. Air-conditioning equipment is optional. Ceiling height, first floor, 8 feet 3 inches; second floor, 8 feet.

Plan No. 406—Size, 36 by 30 feet

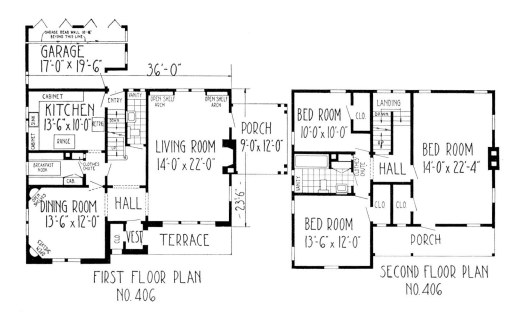

FIRST FLOOR PLAN
NO. 406

SECOND FLOOR PLAN
NO. 406

The Modernistic design with a touch of Southern style combine to produce a really beautiful creation and the effort to originate an exterior effect to combine originality in design with beauty in appearance has well succeeded. Entrance is made through vestibule to hall with arched entrance to living room and to dining room. The living room is spacious and well-lighted and has a fireplace in center with door at side leading to porch, and recessed arches at rear of room with open shelves for ornamental pieces or books. The dining room has recessed corner arches with open shelves. The kitchen has cabinets on both outside walls with sink and window openings in center, chimney for range, breakfast nook adjoining with cabinet and clothes chute, space for refrigerator, and door to rear entry leading to basement and outdoors. The center hall has a lavatory with built-in vanity, and stairway to second floor where three bedrooms and bathroom are provided. The large bedroom has a fireplace and the bathroom has a built-in vanity with linen closet, and a clothes chute is located in hall. The exterior walls are of siding except portion of front wall, which is constructed of common brick, painted white. Seven-foot basement under entire house with ample space for large recreation room, toilet room, laundry, furnace, fruit, vegetable and storage rooms. Hot water heating plant with oil burner equipment is recommended. Air-conditioning equipment may be installed. Double garage in rear with entrance doors at rear or side. Ceiling height, first floor, 8 feet 3 inches; second floor, 8 feet.

Plan No. 415—Size, 44 by 30 feet

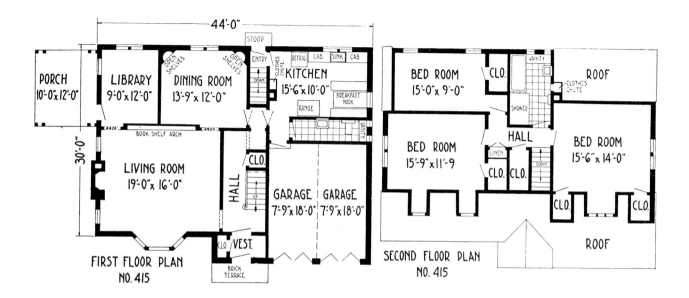

PORCH
10'-0"x 12'-0"

LIBRARY
9'-0"x 12'-0"

DINING ROOM
13'-9"x 12'-0"

STOOP

ENTRY

REFRIG. CAB. SINK CAB.

KITCHEN
15'-6"x 10'-0"

OPEN SHELVES

OPEN SHELVES

CLOTHES CHUTE

DOWN

BREAKFAST NOOK

RANGE

BOOK SHELF ARCH

30'-0"

44'-0"

LIVING ROOM
19'-0"x 16'-0"

CLO.

HALL

UP

VANITY

GARAGE
7'-9"x 18'-0"

GARAGE
7'-9"x 18'-0"

CLO. **VEST.**

BRICK TERRACE

FIRST FLOOR PLAN
NO. 415

BED ROOM
15'-0"x 9'-0"

CLO.

VANITY

SHOWER

CLOTHES CHUTE

ROOF

BED ROOM
15'-9"x 11'-9

LINEN

CLO. CLO.

HALL

DOWN

BED ROOM
15'-6" x 14'-0"

CLO.

CLO.

ROOF

SECOND FLOOR PLAN
NO. 415

A very unique design with buff-color brick for exterior walls, artistic bay window, double garage at side, triple dormers and projected vestibule produces a very pleasing exterior. The vestibule has closet, and leads to hall which has stairway to second floor, closet under stairway, arched opening to rear hall with doors to garage, lavatory, kitchen and dining room. The living room is large and well-lighted and has fireplace, bay window, recessed arch opening in rear wall with open shelves for ornamental pieces or books, with arched openings at either side leading to dining room, and to library which has door to side porch. The kitchen is very roomy and has a breakfast nook, cabinet with sink and window opening in center, refrigerator space, chimney for range, clothes chute, door to hall, from which entry to lavatory and garage is provided, and door to rear entry leading to basement and outdoors. The second floor arrangement includes three bedrooms, hall closet, linen closet, clothes chute, and bathroom with shower and built-in vanity with wall space for mirror between two casement windows. Seven-foot basement under entire house with ample space for large recreation room, toilet, laundry, furnace, fruit, vegetable and storage rooms. Hot water heating plant with oil burner equipment is recommended. Air-conditioning equipment may be installed. Ceiling height, first floor, 8 feet 3 inches; second floor, 8 feet.

Design No. 417

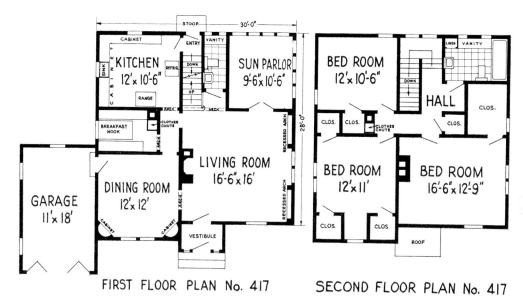

FIRST FLOOR PLAN No. 417   SECOND FLOOR PLAN No. 417

Plan No. 417—Size, 30 by 28 feet

With shingled exterior walls, projected vestibule and portion of garage this cozy appearing semi-bungalow type home is a very popular design. Entrance is made through vestibule into large well-lighted living room, which has a fireplace, arched openings to dining room and over stairway lavatory entrance, and recessed arch openings in side wall with open shelves for books or ornamental pieces. The dining room has recessed corner arches and door to garage. The kitchen has a cabinet with two-tray sink in center, chimney for range, refrigerator space, breakfast nook adjoining with clothes chute, and door to rear entry leading to basement and outdoors. Three bedrooms are provided on second floor, bathroom with built-in vanity, clothes chute and ample closet space for all rooms. Seven-foot basement under entire house with space for recreation room, laundry, furnace, vegetable, toilet and storage rooms. Hot water heating plant with oil burner equipment is recommended. Air-conditioning equipment may be installed. Ceiling height, first floor, 8 feet 3 inches; second floor, 8 feet.

Design No. 439

90

FIRST FLOOR PLAN No. 439   SECOND FLOOR PLAN No. 439

Plan No. 439—Size, 36 by 32 feet

Wide white siding, green painted blinds, bay window projected over attractive design entrance door and screened porch at side combine to produce this stately and artistic exterior. The front vestibule has a coat closet and door to center hall which has triple arched openings to living room, dining room, and rear hall housing stairway, and lavatory with built-in vanity. The living room is good size and well-lighted and has a fireplace, French doors to side porch, and recessed arches across rear wall with open shelves for books and ornamental pieces and French doors in center leading to sunroom. The dining room has recessed corner arches with cabinet space below and open or enclosed shelves at top. The kitchen is very roomy and modern, having cabinets with sink and

window opening in center of one, chimney for range, clothes chute, refrigerator space, breakfast nook adjoining with cabinet, door to two-car garage and door to rear entry leading to basement and outdoors. The second floor arrangement includes four bedrooms, hall closet, linen closet, clothes chute and two bathrooms, each with built-in vanity with wall space for mirror between two casement windows. Seven-foot basement under entire house with ample space for large recreation room, lavatory, laundry, furnace, vegetable, fruit and storage rooms. Hot water heating plant with oil burner equipment is recommended. Air-conditioning equipment optional. Ceiling height, first floor, 8 feet 3 inches; second floor, 8 feet.

Plan No. 412—Size, 40 by 26 feet

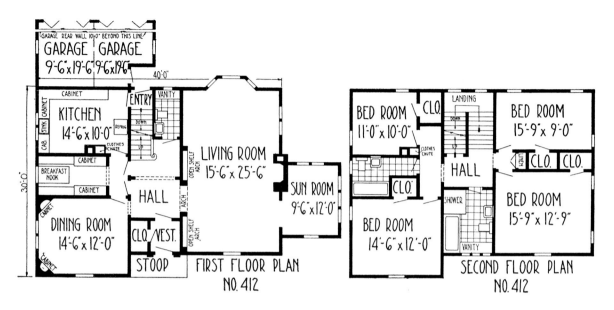

FIRST FLOOR PLAN NO. 412

GARAGE REAR WALL 10'0" BEYOND THIS LINE

GARAGE 9'-6" x 19'-6"
GARAGE 9'-6" x 19'-6"

40'-0"

CABINET
KITCHEN 14'-6" x 10'-0"
SINK CABINET
CAB.
REFRIG.
CLOTHES CHUTE
CABINET
BREAKFAST NOOK
CABINET
ENTRY
VANITY
DOWN
UP
OPEN SHELF ARCH

LIVING ROOM 15'-6" x 25'-6"

SUN ROOM 9'-6" x 12'-0"

30'-0"

CABINET
DINING ROOM 14'-6" x 12'-0"
HALL
CLO. VEST.
ARCH
OPEN SHELF ARCH
STOOP
CABINET

SECOND FLOOR PLAN NO. 412

BED ROOM 11'-0" x 10'-0"
CLO.
LANDING
DOWN
UP
CLOTHES CHUTE
BED ROOM 15'-9" x 9'-0"
CLO.
HALL
LINEN
CLO.
CLO.
BED ROOM 14'-6" x 12'-0"
SHOWER
VANITY
BED ROOM 15'-9" x 12'-9"

The exterior design of this beautiful home is the popular type which will always remain in style. A roomy vestibule with coat closet provides entry to center hall which has a lavatory with built-in vanity, and stairway to second floor. Arched openings lead to dining room and to spacious well-lighted living room, which has a fireplace, French doors to sunroom, bay window at rear, and recessed arches at either side of entrance arch, with open shelves for ornamental pieces or books. The dining room has recessed corner arches with open shelves, to complete a harmonious and beautiful interior. The kitchen has cabinets along outside walls with sink and window opening in center, refrigerator space, chimney for range, clothes chute, breakfast nook adjoining with cabinets, and door to rear entry leading to basement and outdoors, also to double garage. The second floor arrangement includes four bedrooms, each with good size closets, clothes chute, linen closet and two bathrooms. The main bathroom has a shower and built-in vanity with wall space for mirror between two casement windows. Exterior walls are shingled. Seven-foot basement under entire house with ample space for large recreation room, toilet room, laundry, furnace, fruit, vegetable and storage rooms. Hot water heating plant with oil burner equipment is recommended. Air-conditioning equipment may be installed. Ceiling height, first floor, 8 feet 3 inches; second floor, 8 feet.

Design No. 11

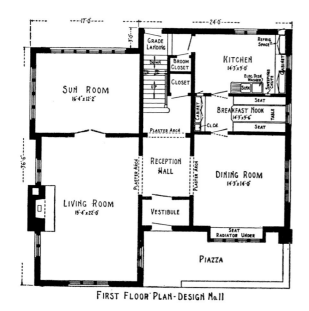

FIRST FLOOR PLAN - DESIGN No. 11

SECOND FLOOR PLAN
DESIGN No. 11

This unusually attractive home is English type; size 36 feet, 6 inches in depth by 41 feet in width. The exterior has a very striking appearance and denotes the very latest in architectural design. Entrance is made through vestibule to reception hall, with artistic plaster arch openings to living room, dining room and adjoining hall with coat closet and staircase leading to second floor. The large living room is exceptionally well-lighted and has an attractive design fireplace, with French doors leading to large bright sunroom. The dining room is good size and is separated from kitchen by a very cheerful breakfast room with table, seats and cabinet. The kitchen is very roomy and equipped with modern fixtures and conveniences, including chute for sweepings, and has a door to rear entry hall, leading to basement and outdoors. Four large chambers are provided on second floor, each with roomy closets. The center hall has a linen closet, clothes chute and connects all rooms. The bathroom is completely equipped, has tile floor and walls and is fitted with hinged seat towel cabinet, shower, and electric heater built in wall. The owner's chamber is very roomy and well-lighted, has gas log fireplace and connecting bathroom. The third floor arrangement provides for maids' room and bath, storage and cedar closets. Seven-foot basement extends under entire house, with large recreation room, boiler, preserve, laundry, toilet and storage rooms.

Design No. 443

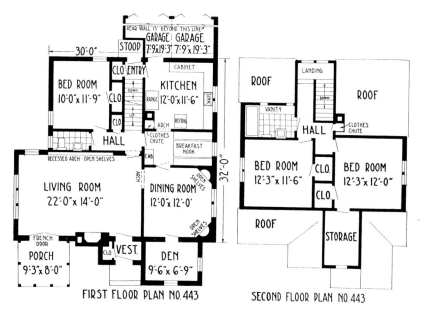

FIRST FLOOR PLAN NO. 443

SECOND FLOOR PLAN NO. 443

Plan No. 443—Size, 30 by 32 feet

The doubled gable front wall of stone and siding, attractive design fireplace chimney and awning-covered glazed porch give this home a rich appearance and individuality in design. The exterior walls are of brick except front wall, which is a combination of stone and siding. The vestibule entry has a coat closet and adjoins large well-lighted living room with fireplace, French doors to porch, arched opening to dining room, recessed arch along rear wall with open shelves for books and ornamental pieces, and door to hall enclosing stairway and lavatory. The kitchen is completely modern, having two cabinets with sink and window opening in center of one, chimney and space for range, space for refrigerator, breakfast nook adjoining with cabinet, door to two-car garage and door to rear entry leading to basement and outdoors. The second floor arrangement includes two additional bedrooms, clothes chute and bathroom with built-in vanity with wall space for mirror between two casement windows. Seven-foot basement under entire house with space for recreation room, toilet, laundry, furnace, vegetable and storage rooms. Hot water heating plant with oil burner equipment is recommended. Air-conditioning equipment optional. Ceiling height, first floor, 8 feet 3 inches; second floor, 8 feet.

Design No. 433

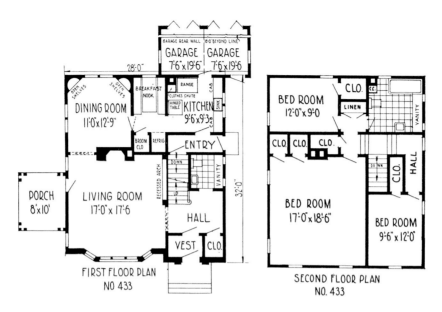

Plan No. 433—Size, 28 by 32 feet

Using common brick, painted white, for lower portion of front wall with shingles above and having front living room wall recessed with bay windows makes a very effective exterior. Entry is made through vestibule to hall, which has a large coat closet, arched opening to living room, stairway to second floor and lavatory with built-in vanity. The living room is large and well lighted and has a fireplace with arched opening at side to dining room, French door to side porch and recessed arch with open shelves for books and ornamental pieces. The dining room has recessed corner arches and swinging door to kitchen. The kitchen is very complete having cabinet with sink and window opening in center, chimney for range, drop table, breakfast nook with broom closet and refrigerator space, door to two-car garage and door to side entry leading to basement and outdoors. The second floor arrangement includes three bedrooms, hall closet, linen closet, clothes chute and large bathroom with built-in vanity and wall space for mirror between two casement windows. Seven-foot basement under entire house with space for recreation room, toilet, laundry, furnace, vegetable and storage rooms. Hot water heating plant with oil burner attachment is recommended. Air-conditioning equipment may be installed. Ceiling height, first floor, 8 feet 3 inches; second floor, 8 feet.

Design No. 138

100

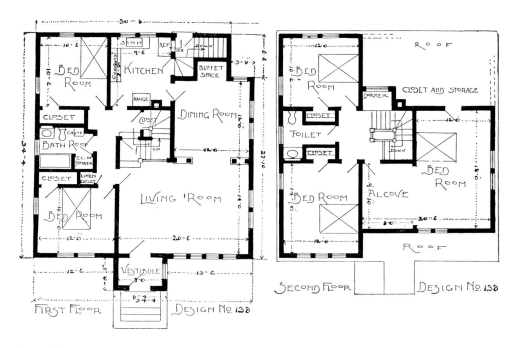

This attractive home, Mission style, is 34 feet 4 inches in width by 34 feet 4 inches in depth. The exterior design is the very latest, and hard to surpass for beauty in appearance. The interior arrangement is very luxurious and palatial. Entrance is made through vestibule, into large and well-lighted living room, which has an artistic arch opening into dining room. Two bedrooms are provided on first floor, connecting with small center hall and bath-room. The kitchen has cupboard, chimney for range, refrigerator space for outside icing, and door to grade landing, leading to basement and outdoors. Three additional bedrooms, and toilet are arranged for on second floor, each with ample closet space. Basement under entire house, fitted with laundry tubs, vegetable cellar and dust-proof coal bin. Hot water heat is recommended. Height of ceilings: first floor, 9 feet; second floor, 8 feet 6 inches.

Design No. 20

FIRST FLOOR PLAN
DESIGN No. 20

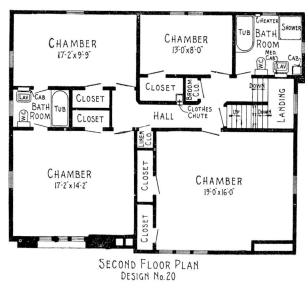

SECOND FLOOR PLAN
DESIGN No. 20

This English type home, size 40 by 31 feet, is strictly the very latest and popular exterior design. Entrance is made through vestibule into large well-lighted living room, which has a fireplace, triple plaster arch opening to dining room, and French door, leading to sunroom. The kitchen is very roomy and provided with all up-to-date conveniences, including chute for sweepings, clothes chute, ample cabinet space, and door to grade landing, leading to basement and outdoors. The second floor arrangement is very compact and includes three large size bedrooms and one smaller size room, each with abundant closet space and connected to center hall and bathroom. Seven-foot basement under entire house, fitted with boiler, laundry, fuel, preserve and recreation rooms.

Design No. 418

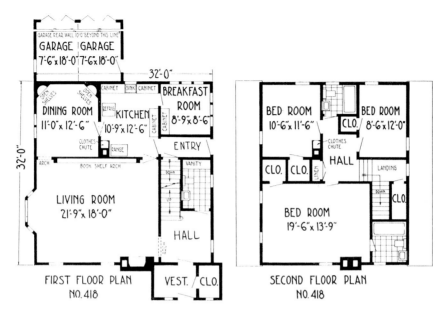

Plan No. 418—Size, 32 by 32 feet

This attractive home with shingled exterior walls, front fireplace, projected vestibule, and sloping roof with dormer on each side from front to rear is a distinctive type and the exterior effect is very pleasing and cozy. The front vestibule has a large closet and leads to hall which has a lavatory with built-in vanity, stairway to second floor, and arched opening to living room which is very spacious and well-lighted and has fireplace in front, bay window at side, a recessed arch opening in rear wall with open shelves for books and ornamental pieces, arched opening to dining room and door to kitchen. The kitchen has a cabinet with sink in center, chimney for range, clothes chute, refrigerator space, breakfast room adjoining, and door to side entry leading to basement and outdoors. A two-car garage is located in rear of house. The second floor arrangement includes a master bedroom with private bathroom adjoining, two other bedrooms and a main bathroom, clothes chute and linen closet. Seven-foot basement under entire house with space for recreation room, toilet, laundry, furnace, vegetable, fruit and storage rooms. Hot water heating plant with oil burner equipment is recommended. Air-conditioning equipment may be installed. Ceiling height, first floor, 8 feet 3 inches; second floor, 8 feet.

Design No. 444

106

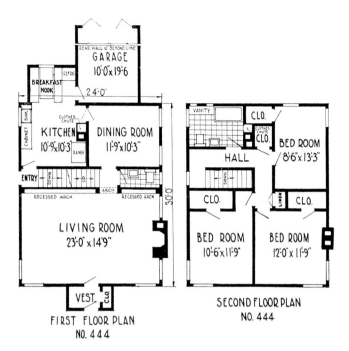

Plan No. 444—Size, 24 by 30 feet

The square type house of siding with corner windows resembling steel constructed houses is very popular and economical to construct. The vestibule entry has a coat closet and adjoins luxurious and well-lighted living room which has a fireplace, recessed arches across rear wall with open shelves for books and ornamental pieces and opening in center to stairway entry with doors to dining room and lavatory. The kitchen has cabinet with sink and window opening, chimney for range, clothes chute, breakfast nook with refrigerator space and door to garage, and doors to dining room and to side entry leading to basement and outdoors. The second floor arrangement includes three bedrooms, hall closet, linen closet and bathroom with clothes chute and built-in vanity with wall space for mirror between two casement windows. Seven-foot basement under entire house with space for recreation room, toilet, laundry, furnace, vegetable and storage rooms. Hot water heating plant with oil burner equipment is recommended. Air-conditioning equipment optional. Ceiling height, first floor, 8 feet 3 inches; second floor, 8 feet.

107

Design No. 8

108

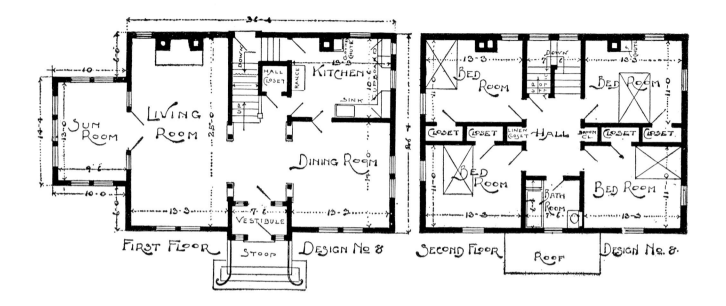

This attractive home of English Colonial architecture is 36 feet in width by 26 feet in depth, exclusive of sunroom. The exterior appearance commands an appearance of stateliness, stability and individuality. The interior with vestibule entrance, reception hall, grand staircase, and arch opening into dining room, also to living room, which has a fireplace and French doors leading to sunroom, all combine in making this a most gorgeous and palatial interior arrangement. The kitchen is provided with large cupboard space, chimney for range, and door to grade landing leading to basement and outdoors. There are four large bedrooms on second floor, each having ample closet space, and connecting to center hall and bathroom. The finish in living room, dining room and hall can be mahogany veneer, oak, finished Old English or silver gray, or birch, stained red or brown mahogany. The sunroom should be of birch, finished old ivory or French gray. The balance of the house can be birch, white enameled, with mahogany stained doors on second floor. Basement under entire house, fitted with storage room, laundry tubs, vegetable cellar, and dust-proof coal bin. Height of ceilings: first floor, 9 feet; second floor, 8 feet.

Design No. 12

110

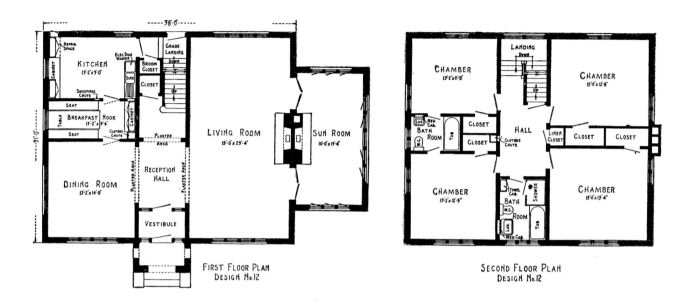

FIRST FLOOR PLAN
DESIGN No. 12

SECOND FLOOR PLAN
DESIGN No. 12

This English Colonial home is a decided departure from the usual type and presents a much richer and more attractive appearance, brought about by the entrance design, stone trim and front gable. The interior arrangement is all that could be desired, with front vestibule entrance, center hall with plaster arch openings to living room, dining room, and grand staircase. The exceptional large living room has a fireplace with French doors on either side, leading to the cheerful sunroom, which also has a fireplace. The dining room is large and well lighted and connects with breakfast room which has table, seats, cabinet and clothes chute. The kitchen is very roomy and fitted with all essentials, including chute for sweepings and door to rear entry hall, leading to basement and outdoors. Four large well-lighted chambers are provided on second floor, each having large closets. The center hall has a clothes chute, linen closet and connects all rooms. The bathroom is good size and well lighted and has tile floor and walls, towel cabinet, shower, and electric heater built in wall. The third floor arrangement includes maids' room and bath, storage and cedar closets. Seven-foot basement under entire house, with large recreation room, laundry, preserve, boiler, toilet and storage rooms. The exterior dimensions are 31 feet in depth by 38 feet in width, exclusive of the sunroom projection.

Design No. 420

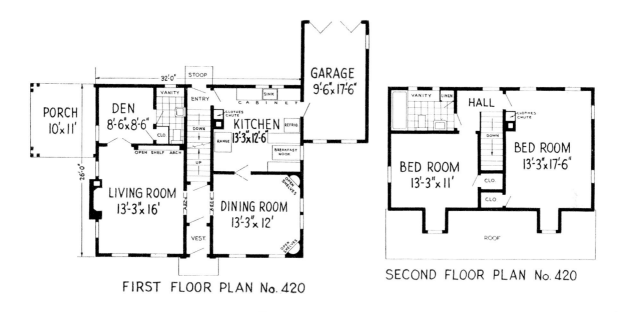

FIRST FLOOR PLAN No. 420

SECOND FLOOR PLAN No. 420

Plan No. 420—Size, 32 by 26 feet

The bungalow type home is always popular and this design with porch and garage at either side has a very pleasing and homelike appearance. Entry is made through vestibule to small center hall with arched openings to living room and to dining room. The living room has a fireplace, French doors to den, and recessed arch opening with open shelves for books or ornamental pieces. The den has a closet, door to side porch and door to lavatory, which has a built-in vanity with wall space for mirror between two casement windows. The kitchen is very complete with a cabinet with two-tray sink in center, clothes chute, chimney for range, refrigerator space, breakfast nook, door to garage and door to rear entry leading to basement and outdoors. Two bedrooms, bathroom and clothes chute are provided on second floor. The bathroom has a linen closet and built-in vanity with wall space for mirror between two casement windows. Seven-foot basement under entire house with space for recreation room, toilet, laundry, vegetable, furnace and storage rooms. Hot water heating plant with oil burner equipment is recommended. Air-conditioning equipment may be installed if desired. Ceiling height, first floor, 8 feet 3 inches; second floor, 8 feet.

113

Design No. 419

114

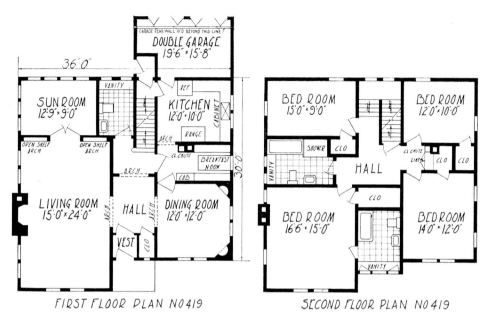

FIRST FLOOR PLAN NO.419

SECOND FLOOR PLAN NO.419

Plan No. 419—Size, 36 by 30 feet

This strictly modern type home with shingled exterior walls is a thoroughly practical design and embodies individuality and richness. Entrance is made through vestibule to center hall which has a clothes closet, and triple arch openings to living room, dining room and rear hall with stairway, and lavatory adjoining. The living room is very spacious and well-lighted and has a fireplace, French doors to sunroom and recessed arch openings at either side with open shelves for books or ornamental pieces. The kitchen has two cabinets, one with sink in center and the other with refrigerator space, chimney for range, breakfast nook adjoining with cabinet and clothes chute, doors to two-car garage at rear and to rear entry leading to basement and outdoors. The second floor arrangement includes a master bedroom with private bathroom adjoining, three other good size bedrooms, main bathroom, clothes chute, and linen closet. Seven-foot basement under entire house with ample space for large recreation room, toilet, laundry, furnace, vegetable and storage rooms. Hot water heating plant with oil burner equipment is recommended. Air-conditioning equipment may be installed if desired. Ceiling height, first floor, 8 feet 3 inches; second floor, 8 feet.

Design No. 94

116

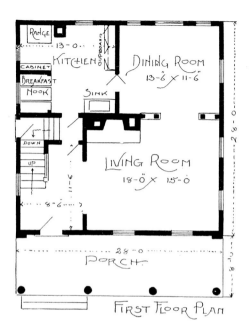

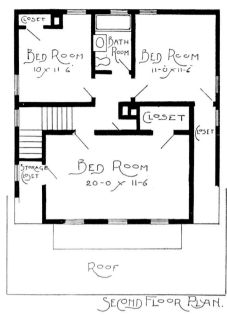

This Colonial style house is 28 feet square. The living room is spacious and has a fireplace, and arch leading into dining room. The kitchen has a cupboard, chimney for range, breakfast nook, and door to grade landing, leading to basement and outdoors. There are three bedrooms on second floor, each with ample closet space, and connecting to center hall and bathroom. An 8-inch brick water table extends around house, with wide lap siding above. If desired, stucco or a combination of brick and stucco can be substituted in place of the lap siding. Basement under entire house, fitted with laundry tubs, vegetable cellar and dust-proof coal bin. Height of ceilings: first floor, 9 feet; second floor, 8 feet.

Design No. 15

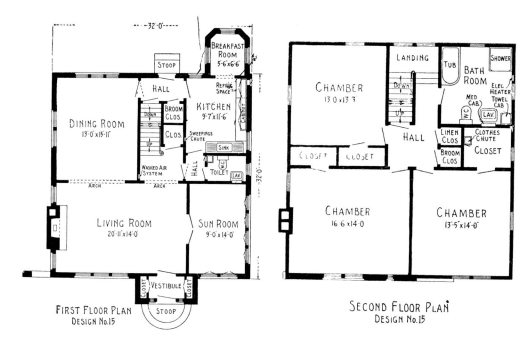

FIRST FLOOR PLAN
DESIGN No.15

SECOND FLOOR PLAN
DESIGN No.15

The projected vestibule entrance, front gable effect, with combination of brick and stucco, all combine in producing this very pleasing and latest style exterior. The house is 32 feet square, exclusive of vestibule and breakfast room projections. The interior arrangement presents a very palatial and homelike appearance, with large well-lighted living room, having fireplace, French doors leading to sunroom and plaster arch openings to dining room and stairway hall. Three good size chambers are provided on second floor, each with roomy closets and connected to center hall and bathroom. The center hall has a linen and broom closet, also stairway leading to third floor where there is ample space for maids' room and bath, cedar and storage closets. Seven-foot basement under entire house, fitted with laundry, boiler, vegetable, and recreation rooms.

119

Design No. 438

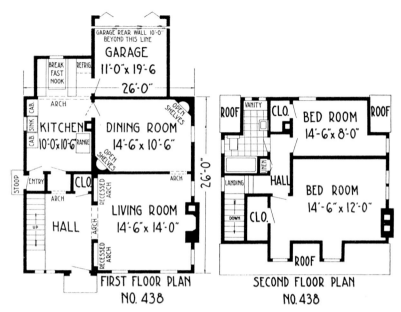

FIRST FLOOR PLAN
NO. 438

SECOND FLOOR PLAN
NO. 438

Plan No. 438—Size, 26 by 26 feet

This neat appearing cottage type home has all the conveniences found in expensive homes and considering exterior dimensions a good many good size rooms are provided. The exterior walls are covered with shingles. The entrance door is recessed and leads to hall with open staircase, coat closet, arched openings to living room and kitchen. The living room has a fireplace, arched opening to dining room and recessed arches with open shelves for books and ornamental pieces. The dining room has recessed corner arches with cabinet space below and open or enclosed shelves above. The kitchen has a cabinet with sink and window opening in center, chimney for range, breakfast nook with refrigerator space and door to garage, and doors to front hall and to side entry leading to basement and outdoors. The second floor arrangement includes two bedrooms, linen closet and bathroom with built-in vanity with wall space for mirror between two casement windows. Seven-foot basement under entire house with space for recreation room, toilet, laundry, furnace, vegetable and storage rooms. Warm air or hot water heating plant may be used with oil burner equipment. Air-conditioning equipment optional. Ceiling height, first floor, 8 feet 3 inches; second floor, 8 feet.

PRICE LIST
of Complete Working Plans, Details and Specifications

Plan Number	Pages	Cubic Foot Content	Price of Plans	Plan Number	Pages	Cubic Foot Content	Price of Plans
1	4–5	39,429	$25.00	417	88–89	26,988	15.50
7	22–23	42,981	26.00	418	104–105	32,256	18.75
8	108–109	33,166	19.00	419	114–115	35,220	20.50
11	94–95	43,989	27.25	420	112–113	23,044	13.75
12	110–111	44,811	27.25	421	24–25	26,546	15.50
15	118–119	35,162	21.00	422	8–9	30,346	17.00
17	14–15	33,694	19.00	423	80–81	26,167	16.00
20	102–103	41,540	25.00	424	50–51	49,108	28.75
22	12–13	32,975	19.75	425	10–11	23,912	15.00
36	6–7	29,240	16.50	426	40–41	25,962	15.25
52	28–29	32,104	18.25	427	66–67	28,182	17.00
74	20–21	28,140	16.00	428	2–3	25,507	15.25
94	116–117	24,304	15.00	429	72–73	25,165	15.00
138	100–101	31,745	18.00	430	58–59	29,280	18.00
401	68–69	32,760	20.00	431	34–35	26,696	15.75
402	38–39	29,484	18.00	432	42–43	27,924	16.50
403	78–79	30,639	18.50	433	98–99	28,224	17.25
404	46–47	36,506	20.50	434	16–17	43,629	26.00
405	30–31	32,605	19.25	435	18–19	35,282	21.75
406	84–85	27,334	17.50	436	74–75	32,147	18.75
407	60–61	27,291	16.25	437	64–65	26,014	16.25
408	36–37	43,189	25.00	438	120–121	20,767	12.25
409	52–53	41,477	23.25	439	90–91	35,136	21.00
410	62–63	33,633	20.50	440	56–57	31,883	19.75
411	76–77	43,729	27.50	441	82–83	25,169	14.50
412	92–93	38,061	22.25	442	32–33	22,736	14.25
413	70–71	25,783	15.25	443	96–97	30,527	18.75
414	44–45	28,534	17.50	444	106–107	21,792	13.00
415	86–87	30,022	18.75	445	48–49	22,856	13.50
416	54–55	28,290	17.50	446	26–27	30,240	18.00

The prices quoted on the previous page are for one complete set of plans, details and specifications.

ADDITIONAL SETS OF PLANS, INCLUDING DETAILS . . . . $3.50 per set
ADDITIONAL SETS OF SPECIFICATIONS . . . . $1.00 per set

COMPLETE PLANS include blue prints of front, rear and both side elevations, wall section, basement plan including section of foundation wall, also complete floor plans, all drawn to a scale of one-quarter inch to the foot.

DETAILS include blue prints of arches, fireplace, bookcases, breakfast nook, kitchen cabinet, doors, staircase, moldings and all interior trim, drawn to a scale of one inch to the foot. The various fixtures are shown in two or three styles, affording you a choice in design.

SPECIFICATIONS include from ten to twelve typewritten pages and are complete in every particular, covering all products required, the kind and quality, and the manner in which the labor is to be performed.

PLANS AND SPECIFICATIONS

Exterior Material

If desired, lumber (siding or shingles), stucco, brick veneer, hollow tile and brick, or a combination of either may be substituted in place of the specific material shown in illustration, without making any change in plans. A 12-inch foundation wall provides for use of any of these materials. If hollow tile and brick is used, the outside dimensions of building should be increased eight inches in length and width, four inches on all sides, to retain the same inside measurements as shown in floor plan illustration. A detail sheet is furnished with each set of plans, showing the exact method of construction, with use of any of the materials above mentioned.

Interior Changes

Changes in arrangement of interior fixtures, such as eliminating or adding fireplace, substituting French doors or plain cased openings in place of arches, eliminating or adding certain fixtures or cabinets, or omitting kitchen chimney, can be arranged for at owner's will, by noting changes in writing and incorporating same in specifications and contract.

Alterations in Plans

When the alterations desired require only the changing of partitions or slight rearrangement of rooms, lengthening or diminishing size of building, changing location or size of windows and doors, it is not necessary to have such changes shown on the blue prints, but if changes are desired, such as will require redrawing of plans (refer to following paragraph).

Special Plans

If you do not find a design in this book to serve your purpose and desire to have a special set of drawings prepared, simply mail us a rough pencil sketch of the arrangement wanted and we will promptly quote you our most reasonable rate for preparing the special plans.

Location

The homes illustrated in this book are suitable for erection in any locality. In sections where the climate is warm the year round, and where full basement under entire house is not required, the foundation plan is used in the same manner, to provide for basement under any certain portion of house, and for correct wall footing, if no basement at all is required.

Instructions for Ordering Plans

When ordering plans, kindly enclose remittance in full, with order. If you desire to have plans reversed (a transposition of the rooms, from one side to the other), be sure and mention when ordering. Plans will be shipped same day as order is received.